Advance Praise for *Lauren Ipsum*

"A Looking Glass tale for the computer age."
—*School Library Journal*

"Part of a much larger movement that seeks to bring programming skills to, well, everyone."
—*Wired*

"Captures the spirit of problem solving and ignites readers' imaginations . . . introduces girls and boys to computer science—and to a new way of thinking and problem solving."
—SHERYL SANDBERG, FACEBOOK COO AND AUTHOR OF *Lean In*

"An enchanting fable that just happens to be grounded in fundamental concepts of computation."
—JOCELYN GOLDFEIN, FORMER DIRECTOR OF ENGINEERING AT FACEBOOK

"A fantastical journey into the 21st century tech 'Wonderland' that both educates and entertains."
—RUTHE FARMER, CHIEF STRATEGY & GROWTH OFFICER, NATIONAL CENTER FOR WOMEN & IT

"*Lauren Ipsum* is a wonderful guide to the ideas behind computing. I wish I'd had her as a friend when I was growing up."
—DR. ROBERT ST. AMANT, AUTHOR OF *Computing for Ordinary Mortals*

"A must-read for anyone looking to spice up their learning or teaching of computer science."
—DR. HÉLÈNE MARTIN, UNIVERSITY OF WASHINGTON

"Sheds a positive light on computing for those who might otherwise miss out."
—GAIL CARMICHAEL, CARLETON UNIVERSITY FACULTY & BOARD ADVISOR FOR THE ANITA BORG INSTITUTE FOR WOMEN AND TECHNOLOGY

LAUREN iPSUM

A STORY ABOUT COMPUTER SCIENCE AND OTHER IMPROBABLE THINGS

CARLOS BUENO

no starch
press

SAN FRANCISCO

LAUREN IPSUM. Copyright © 2015 by Carlos Bueno.

Printed in USA

First printing

18 17 16 15 14   1 2 3 4 5 6 7 8 9

ISBN-10: 1-59327-574-9
ISBN-13: 978-1-59327-574-7

Publisher: William Pollock
Production Editor: Riley Hoffman
Cover Design: Beth Middleworth
Illustrator: Miran Lipovača
Developmental Editor: Jennifer Griffith-Delgado
Copyeditor: Rachel Monaghan
Compositor: Riley Hoffman
Proofreader: Paula L. Fleming

For information on distribution, translations, or bulk sales, please contact No Starch Press, Inc. directly:

No Starch Press, Inc.
245 8th Street, San Francisco, CA 94103
phone: 415.863.9900; info@nostarch.com
www.nostarch.com

Library of Congress Cataloging-in-Publication Data
Bueno, Carlos, 1979-
   Lauren Ipsum : a story about computer science and other improbable things / Carlos Bueno.
      pages cm
   Summary: Lauren, a clever girl lost in Userland, applies logic and problem solving skills to find her way home, encountering along the way such concepts as timing attacks, algorithm design, and the traveling salesman problem.
   ISBN 978-1-59327-574-7 -- ISBN 1-59327-574-9
   [1. Computer science--Fiction. 2. Problem solving--Fiction. 3. Fantasy.] I. Title.
   PZ7.1.B84Lau 2014
   [Fic]--dc23
                                2014035552

The Computers in This Book

I feel I should warn you: You won't find any computers in this book. If the idea of a computer science book without computers upsets you, please close your eyes until you've finished reading the rest of this page.

The truth is that computer science isn't really about the computer. The computer is just a tool to help you see ideas more clearly. You can see the moon and stars without a telescope, smell the flowers without a fluoroscope, have fun without a funoscope, and be silly sans oscilloscope.

You can also play with computer science without you-know-what. Ideas are the real stuff of computer science. This book is about those ideas and how to find them. In fact, most of the characters, places, and thingamajigs in Userland are actually based on those ideas. Check out the Field Guide at the back of the book to learn more about them!

Contents

CHAPTER 0   Mostly Lost 1

CHAPTER 1   A Hidden Ally 11

CHAPTER 2   Sense and Sensibleness. 15

CHAPTER 3   Rounding Error 21

CHAPTER 4   What the Tortoise Said to Laurie 27

CHAPTER 5   Welcome to Symbol 35

CHAPTER 6   A Tinker's Trade 41

CHAPTER 7   Read Me. 55

CHAPTER 8   More Than One Way to Do It 61

CHAPTER 9   Don't Repeat Yourself 67

CHAPTER 10   A Well-Timed Entrance. 71

CHAPTER 11   A Fair Exchange 75

CHAPTER 12   An Improbable Twist. 79

CHAPTER 13   The Game of Life 85

CHAPTER 14   In the Abstract. 91

CHAPTER 15   Cleverness When It Counts 99

CHAPTER 16   A Change of Plan. 113

CHAPTER 17   Chasing Elegants. 121

CHAPTER 18   Many Hands Make Light Work 131

CHAPTER 19   Branching Out. 137

CHAPTER 20   Fin 147

CHAPTER 21   One More Thing. 151

The Field Guide to Userland 155

CHAPTER 0

Mostly Lost

Lauren Ipsum had been lost in the woods all morning. The poor girl didn't know where she was or where she was going.

It had all started with an argument. Her mother wanted her to go to summer school, and naturally Laurie didn't want to go. "Children in other countries go to school year round," her mom said. "We aren't in other countries," Laurie replied. "Extra classes are how to get ahead," Mom said. "Summer is for having fun," Laurie insisted. The argument went on and on and got loud near the end. To calm down, Laurie took a walk in the woods.

When people are faced with something they don't want to do, they often do something they aren't allowed to do instead. Before long, Laurie had gone farther into the woods than she had ever gone before.

Being lost was kind of fun. Out here, Laurie could be anything she wanted to be, and there was no one to tell her different.

She was a secret ninja, moving like a ghost through the ancient forest. Light and shadow danced under the leaves, and she danced with them. No one could hear her stealthy ninja footsteps. No one would see her coming until it was too—

"*Chiguire!*" said a voice up ahead. A shape came toward her out of the darkness. Was it an angry spirit? A dire beast?

"*Argot!*" the creature said. It was like a mouse-dog, or a dog-mouse. That is to say, it was the size of a dog, but it looked more like a mouse. It walked right up to Laurie and began nuzzling her hand in a very un-beast-like way.

"Aw, you're so friendly!" Laurie said, in a rather un-ninja-like fashion.

"*Repl!*" it said, as it put a webbed foot on her knee.

"You're a funny-looking thing, aren't you? What's your name, huh? What should I call you?"

"*Argot!*"

"Okay, I'll call you Argot. Are you hungry? What do . . . things like you eat?" She offered it some peanuts.

"*Snarfl!*" it snarfled, eating out of her hand.

"Hey, little guy," she said, tickling its chin, "you don't know the way back to Hamilton, do you?"

"*Hamilton!*" it said excitedly.

"You do know a way?"

"*Lalr!*" it lalred, tongue hanging out.

"So where is it?"

"*Isit!*" it said.

"I mean, how do I get there?"

"*Gether!*" it answered.

"You're just repeating what I'm saying, aren't you?"

"*Arentyou!*" it said.

"That's what I thought. Animals can't talk."

So now I'm lost, Laurie thought to herself. *How do I get unlost?* She remembered something about moss growing on the north side of trees. There wasn't any moss, so that was out. *The sun rises in the east and sets in the west.* It was late morning, and the sun was almost overhead. No help there either.

She wandered around, flipping her lucky red poker chip. If the chip landed on heads, she walked to the left for a while. If it landed on tails, she walked to the right for a while.

"*Burble . . .*" Argot waddled behind her, making nonsense noises.

"No, don't follow me, Argot. Shoo!"

"*Bitblit?*"

"I like you, but I'm not allowed to have a dog. Or a mouse, or a dog-mouse, or whatever you are. Go along now—go home!"

No matter what she said, the ugly little thing wouldn't give up. It seemed willing to follow Laurie all the way to . . . wherever she was going.

Maybe if I wait for the stars to come out, she thought to herself. *No, that's silly. I don't know which stars are which!*

"*Frobit!*" Another creature like Argot, but bigger, came out of the underbrush. It tried to lick her face.

"Ugh, your breath stinks!"

"*Wibble!*" A third creature came up from behind and butted its head against her.

"Whoops! Hello to you, too."

"*Tanstaafl!*"

"*Zork!*"

More creatures were coming from all directions. The noise was getting louder.

"Uh," Laurie uhhed.

"*Parsec!*"

"*Wurfl!*"

"*Lilo!*"

Argot's friends were no longer just nuzzling. They were crowding all around her, pushing and shouting. She was being mobbed.

Laurie panicked and ran. The gang of creatures howled and chased after her.

"*Nyquist!*"

"*Quux!*"

"*Fifo!*"

She could barely stay on her feet, running through the tangled underbrush, but she was too afraid to slow down.

Her escape was blocked by a tall green hedge that stretched in both directions. Once upon a time it might have been part of a garden, but now it was wild and disorderly. Laurie squeezed her way through a gap in the hedge and kept running until she thought she was safe. The creatures were far behind.

The forest looked different on the other side of the hedge. For one, the trees had red and black stripes. Black tree trunks split into two red branches. Those split into four black branches, which split into eight red branches, and on and on, until the branches ended in millions of tiny black leaves. In fact . . .

"*Foo!*"

"*Bar!*"

"*Baz!*"

The creatures were still chasing her! Laurie tried to run away again, but she couldn't go very fast. Her throat was raw, and her legs were beginning to tremble.

"*Wysiwyg!*"

"Help! Stop it!" she cried, hoping someone would hear her. "Make them stop!"

A small man carrying a large pack stepped in between Laurie and the mob. Dishes and pots and pans and cowbells rattled around. The creatures halted a few paces away, making awful, angry noises.

"Are you okay, miss?" he said.

"These—these *mouse-dogs* won't leave me alone!"

"*Epsilon!*"

"*Olap!*"

"It's just a bunch of Jargon," he said. "Hold still and stay calm." He cupped his hands to his mouth.

"STANI!" he shouted at them.

All of the Jargon froze, their ears aquiver.

"CEPAT! AFVIGE! *SCHNELL! SCHNELL!*"

And just like that, they were gone, running away into the gloom of the forest.

Laurie collapsed against a tree. "Th-thank you," she said.

"Sure thing, miss. Just rest here a while," the man said. He dropped his pack with a loud jangle, then sat on top of it.

"What's a Jargon?" she asked once she'd caught her breath.

"Jargon live in the swamps. They feed on attention. If they can't get that, they'll settle for fear and confusion."

"But the first one was so friendly! I just talked to it a little and it started following me."

"That's how it starts," he said. "A little Jargon doesn't look like much. Some people even keep them as pets. But they form packs, and they are very dangerous."

"That's terrible!"

He shrugged. "What can you do? Stand your ground and act confident. If you show any fear, a pack of wild Jargon will run you right over."

"What did you say to make them leave?"

"I have no idea. It sounded good, though, didn't it?" he said. "So what's your name, miss?"

"My name is Laurie. I think I'm lost."

"That's wonderful!" the man said. "I'm lost too."

"Oh no! You mean you don't know where you are?"

"No, I know exactly where I am."

"So you don't know where you're going?"

"I know exactly where I'm going. I'm on the way home."

Laurie was almost too confused to feel confused. "But if you know where you *are*," she said, "and you know where you're *going*, how can you be lost?"

"Because I don't know how I'll get there," the man grinned. "I'm a Wandering Salesman."

"A Wandering Salesman? What's that?"

"We wander from town to town, selling and buying. There are two rules: you have to visit every town before going home, and you can't visit any town twice. Every road is the road home except the road behind me."

"So you always go to the next place you've never been to?" she asked.

"That's right! You're guaranteed to get home eventually," he said. "It's only logical. Along the way I've seen the sunrise over the Towers of Hanoi and climbed the Upper Bounds. I've sat down at the Lookup Table and floated on the Overflow River. It's a good life. Being lost can be fun!"

"It's not fun for me anymore," said Laurie. "I don't really know where I am, or where I'm going, *or* how to get there."

"Hmm. Mostly lost is fun, but completely lost is serious. You're going home too, right?"

"Yes, I want to go home!" she said.

"And where do you live?"

"I live in Hamilton with my mom. Do you know where it is?"

"Not a clue. Never heard of it!" he said cheerfully. "But that's one out of three, anyway. You have a definite goal."

"Um, I guess so."

"And I know where *I* am, and since we're in the same place, that means I know where *you* are. You are in the Red-Black Forest, near Mile Zero."

The what near who? she thought to herself, but the man was still talking.

" . . . now you know where you are and where you are going!" the Salesman said. "You are only *mostly* lost."

"But I still don't know how to get there!"

"Hmm," he hmmed, thinking it over. "I know someone you should talk to: a wise lady named Eponymous Bach."

"Where is she?"

"She lives in Bach Haus at the end of Bach Way, in the town of—"

"Bach?"

"How did you guess? Bach is an excellent Composer. At the very least, she can name your problem."

That sounded like a much better plan than waiting for moss to grow!

"Okay, I'll do it. Will you go with me?"

"I would love to, Laurie. But I've just come from visiting Bach," said the Salesman.

"Oh. That means you can't go back, right?"

"Right. I can take you up to the road, but from there you are on your own."

The Wandering Salesman showed her the way to the edge of the forest. Just past the last tree was a road sign. "Ah, here we are," he said. "Route One, Mile Zero."

"I've never seen a Mile *Zero*," said Laurie.

"Everything has to start somewhere. It may not look like much, but this is a very special place. You might even say it's the starting point of the whole System."

"What comes after Mile Zero?"

"Mile One, of course. And right after that is the town of Bach. Are you ready?"

"Yes, I think so. Thank you!"

"You're welcome, Laurie. Good luck! Maybe our paths will cross again." The Wandering Salesman headed off, cowbells and pans rattling, to a place he'd never been before.

And so did Laurie.

CHAPTER 1

A Hidden Ally

"That wasn't *too* bad," Laurie said to herself, as she reached the Mile One sign. "A mile sounds like a long way to walk, but it's easier if you break it into pieces." She remembered that in Hamilton there are eight blocks to a mile, so she made herself think about walking one block at a time.

"Oh, look, another one," said a voice.

"Hello?" Laurie spun around, but there wasn't much to see: some fields of odd-looking crops, an empty road, and the sign.

"She's kind of short, isn't she?"

That's when she noticed a tiny lizard clinging to the sign. It had the oddest coloring: where the sign was green, the lizard was reddish; where it was white, the lizard was black.

"Hello, who are you?" she asked.

"I'm Xor," the lizard squeaked. His tail twitched from yellow to blue. "Hold on, can you *see* me?"

"Of course I can see you!" Laurie said.

"Oh." Xor looked very sad and blushed a bright purple.

"You *are* the first talking lizard I've ever met," Laurie said. "How did you learn to talk?"

"What a silly question!" the creature said. "I learned as a baby, like everybody else."

"You did?"

"Sure. Why, how did *you* learn to talk?"

"Well . . . " She had always been able to talk, hadn't she? "I guess I learned as a baby too."

"It's only logical. First you learn to talk, then you learn to think. Too bad it's not the other way around."

"What are you doing there on the sign?" Laurie asked.

"Another silly question! What does it look like I'm doing? I am blending into the background," Xor said. At that moment he turned pink and violet. "Did you say something?"

She shook her head.

"Where was I? Oh, yes. Blending in is an honorable and ancient art. It takes years of practice. You must have a pretty sharp eye to spot me." Xor marched around the sign as he talked, turning white with large orange polka dots.

Laurie bit her tongue, trying not to laugh.

"No, you don't see a lizard like me every day!" He turned peach and cornflower blue. "But sometimes—personally speaking between you and me, of course—sometimes . . . " He looked sad again and fell silent.

"Sometimes what?"

"Sometimes, I worry I'm not doing it right."

"Not if you want to *hide*!" Laurie said, unable to contain herself. "Your colors keep changing."

"I was pretty sure I'd figured it out this time," Xor said, turning his head around to get a better look at himself.

"My left leg is green—" he said.

"Green? No, it's red."

"Really?"

"Really. Now it's purple."

Xor sighed. "Blending in is a lot harder than it looks. I'm glad it was you who saw me and not a hungry bird. You see, I'm a bit color-blind."

"What kind of lizard are you, anyway?" she asked.

"I'm Chameleon, mostly. I'm part dinosaur on my mother's side."

"Part *dinosaur*? That's impossible."

"It's true!" Xor drew his little self up proudly. "For instance, my Aunt Vana is a Steganosaurus. She can hide anywhere, even on the back of a postage stamp."

Laurie wasn't sure she believed Xor, but she didn't want to hurt the lizard's feelings.

"Maybe your aunt can teach you how to hide better."

"I'd love that. But I don't know where she is. The last time I saw her, I didn't even see her!" he said.

"But—"

"*Hey*," Xor said, "why don't I come along with *you*? If you can see me, maybe you'll be able to see her, too."

"I don't think—"

"It'll be fine! I know a lot about this place. I can show you around."

"Well, okay. I can carry you in my pocket," Laurie said. "Have you heard of Hamilton?"

"I don't know. Can you eat it?"

"Never mind. Let's go."

CHAPTER 2

Sense and Sensibleness

Laurie and Xor soon reached the little town of Bach. It was very confusing at first, because the name "Bach" appeared on everything: Bach Street, Bach Avenue, Bach Plaza—even the sidewalk was labeled *sidebach*. They finally found Bach Haus down Bach Way.

Laurie knocked on the enormous front door. A tall lady with frizzy white hair and an elegant coat answered. "Hello, what can I do for you?" she asked.

"Are you Eponymous Bach? I'm Laurie. I was told you can help me."

"If I can't help solve your problem, I can at least give it a name. Do come in and have some tea."

The house was impressive on the outside, but on the inside it was a mess! Strange machines were shoved against the walls, cobwebs hung down from the corners, tools were scattered on the floor, and piles and piles of paper with scribbled

notes were everywhere. A violin was stuffed into a flowerpot. Xor jumped out of Laurie's pocket to hunt some insects.

"Um, so you're a composer?" Laurie asked.

"That's right," said Eponymous.

"What kind of music do you compose?"

"Oh, I don't compose music," Eponymous said. "I Compose Ideas!"

"You compose . . . ideas? How?"

"I put little ideas together to make bigger ones. Then I put *those* ideas together to make bigger and bigger ones! And then I put my name on them. You shouldn't let any ideas escape without a name," she said. "That's Bach's First Law of Eponymy. I made it myself, you see."

"Is that why all the streets are named after you?" Laurie asked.

"Yes, I used to put my name on Things. But it's much better to have your name on an Idea. That's my Second Law of Eponymy."

"But why is an idea better?" Laurie asked. "You can't see an idea."

"Because good ideas never wear out! You put your name on a birthday cake, but it doesn't last very long, does it?"

"No. You eat it right away," Laurie said. Birthday cakes don't last long at all!

"You can also put your name on a mountain," said Eponymous. "But even a mountain falls down eventually. It makes a terrible noise, too! No, the best way to make something last forever is to take away everything but the ideas." She pointed to a portrait of a man with curly hair and a funny coat. "Look over there," she said.

"That's my friend Andy Ampère. One day, he noticed that when he put electricity through two wires, they would bend a little toward each other. So he called it Andy's Magical Wire Bender, and he went around selling it to people who make paper clips."

"That's pretty neat!" said Laurie.

"Yes, but I told Andy to keep going, to take away all of the Things until he had an Idea worth putting his name on. He realized he could use his machine to measure electricity by looking at how much the wires bent. That was truly new—a new law of nature. Nobody uses Andy's Magical Wire Bender anymore, but Ampère's Law will always be current."

"But why do you put your name on everything?"

"Names are very important! A thing without a name is like a pot without a handle. Just try telling a story about turtles without using the word *turtle*."

"Well," said Laurie, always ready to argue a point, "you could say *a Green Round animal with a Shell* instead of *turtle*."

"Hrmph," Eponymous hrmphed, "That's not a very easy name, but I suppose it will do. So how can I help you, child?"

"I'm looking for a path back to Hamilton. The Wandering Salesman said I just have to go everywhere I've never been before, and eventually I'll find my way home. But . . . "

"But what, dear?"

"I don't know, something about what he said doesn't make sense."

"It might make *sense*, but it may not be *sensible*," said Eponymous.

"Isn't that the same thing?" asked Laurie.

"Many things make sense but are not sensible at all! You can go from the front door to the back door by walking through the house, right?"

"Sure."

"You can also walk around the outside of the house, or even all the way around the planet, to do the same thing. Many ways make sense, but only some are sensible."

"Then I want to find a sensible way," said Laurie. "I don't want to walk all around the planet!"

"So," Eponymous said, "we have named and framed your problem: Laurie's Quest is to find the shortest path home."

"But how do I do that?" asked Laurie. "Is it difficult?"

"You'll never know unless you try. The next town up the road is called Symbol. Have you been there before?"

"No, I've never even heard of it."

"Then it sounds perfect. Just follow Bach Avenue out of town, and take a left at Recursion Junction."

"That's great!" said Laurie. "Xor, let's go. Oh, that's right," she remembered. "Do you know anything about how to find Steganosauruses?"

Eponymous smiled. "Who's been telling you stories like that, my dear girl? Steganosauruses don't exist."

CHAPTER 3

Rounding Error

As they headed out of Bach, Laurie couldn't help but tease Xor a little. "Steganosauruses don't exist, huh?"

"That lady doesn't know what she's talking about. Her place had some really good bugs, though."

"Maybe she's right."

"She says Steganosauruses don't exist because she's never seen one. But that proves my point! Steganosauruses are so good at hiding that people think they're imaginary."

"That doesn't make any sense, Xor."

"Who are you going to believe, me or your own eyes?"

Squawk! Laurie felt something brush her shoulder. Before she knew it, a fat bird was flying away with Xor in its talons.

"*Hey!*" Laurie ran after the bird as it slowly flew to a nearby branch. It was so fat it was almost spherical, about the size and shape of a coconut. There were two more just like it in the tree.

Laurie jumped at the bird holding Xor, but it tossed the lizard to another bird, which caught him in its beak. She jumped at that one, but then Xor was thrown to another.

The birds enjoyed playing keepaway. When their mouths weren't full of lizard, they hopped up and down and sang a silly rhyme:

"Faster and faster—"

"—too fast to follow—"

"—Round Robins throw faster—"

"—than an unladen swallow!"

"Give him back!" Laurie shouted. "He's my friend!" The Round Robins only cackled and mocked her.

"Give him back!"

"Give him back!"

"We think he will make—"

"—an afternoon snack!"

"Help!" Xor squeaked in terror. "They want to eat me!"

"Thought he was hiding—"

"—but bird eyes can see—"

"—an evenly dividing—"

"—meal for three!"

"No!" Laurie picked up a stone and threw it at the nearest Round Robin. To her utter surprise, it didn't fly away. The fat, nasty thing *caught the stone.*

"A stone!"

"How rude!"

"Hardly a treasure."

"We'll happily juggle it—"

"—for your pleasure!"

They played catch with the stone and Xor. Laurie threw another stone, and then another, but the birds caught those, too. Now the Round Robins were juggling three stones plus Xor. This wasn't getting Laurie anywhere. She paused, thinking, another stone in her hand.

"Gave up so soon?"

"We love to play ball!"

"Throw us more toys—"

"—and we'll catch them all!"

Instead of throwing the single stone, Laurie scooped up a large handful and started tossing them in nice, easy lobs, one by one. The Robins caught each stone and juggled it. If they hadn't been trying to eat her friend, Laurie would have been impressed.

"What are you doing? Save me!" Xor said.

Soon, the three Robins were having trouble keeping so many things in the air. Laurie threw the stones harder and faster, trying to knock the birds off balance. They sang for reinforcements.

"More wings, my brothers!"

"More beaks and more talons!"

"We need more Round Robins—"

"—to evenly balance!"

Five more of the creatures flapped and flopped in to join the party of their murderous kin. They evened out the load of stones and mocked Laurie even more loudly.

"You can't beat us that way!"

"We'll have our meal!"

"Each one will eat less—"

"—but a deal's a deal!"

The birds were juggling 15, 20, 25 stones now. They could catch whatever Laurie threw at them, and a dozen more of the creatures were waiting to join in. How could she get Xor away from them?

"Clever Round Robins,"

"too many to beat!"

"You can't stop the Robins—"

"—when there's dinner to eat!"

It was hard to concentrate with the birds singing and Xor screaming, but Laurie waited again, trying to see a pattern. A Round Robin can catch anything. . . .

"'Round he goes!"

"Where will he stop?"

"Stones all a-juggle,"

"but the lizard won't—*mmph!*"

Just as one of the birds was about to catch Xor, Laurie hit it in the beak with a nice big clod of dirt. A Round Robin can catch anything. But it can't catch *two* things!

She caught Xor as he fell and ran away as fast as she could. Stones and furious Robins flew everywhere as the flock lost its rhythm. Some tried to chase her, but they were too fat to keep up and too angry to rhyme.

"No fair!"

"No fair!"

"You stole our snack!"

"Come back!"

"No fair!"

"You stole . . . "

"Are you okay?" Laurie said.

"No . . . yes . . . maybe." Xor was breathing hard. They both were. The little lizard didn't look hurt, but he was scared out of his wits. "Birds!"

"This is why you have to blend in, isn't it?" she asked. "Birds want to eat you."

"I hate birds."

CHAPTER 4

What the Tortoise Said to Laurie

Laurie took a left turn at the sign marked "Recursion Junction." After cresting a little hill, she ended up at . . . Recursion Junction!

"Is this the same place, Xor?" Laurie asked. "It looks like it."

"Try a right turn," he said.

She did, but after a short while they were back where they started. When she tried a second, and a third, and twenty-seventh time, they always came back to Recursion Junction.

"It seems as though I am going somewhere else, but we always come back to the same place. What's going on?" Laurie wondered.

They went around . . .

. . . and around . . .

. . . and around . . .

. . . and around so many times that Laurie lost count. Just as she was about to give up, there was a gigantic smashing sound, like a stack of plates falling to the floor.

They both jumped in fright, and for a moment Xor accidentally turned the same color as Laurie's shirt. They looked around for the source of the noise but couldn't find it. To their surprise, the next turn put them on a different road.

This road was neat and straight, and it seemed to stretch on forever. Up ahead, a man in a Greek helmet was riding on a large Round Green animal with a Shell. (Eponymous might have called the creature a *turtle*, though she wouldn't have been quite right.) The two were moving slowly and steadily away.

"Hey! Wait!" Laurie shouted, running up to them.

"At last, someone has caught up to us!" said the animal.

"I thought that was *impossible*," said the man.

"Hello!" the animal said to Laurie. "I am Tortoise, a humble tortoise." He was much too large to be a mere *turtle*. "This is my esteemed companion, Achilles the Logician."

"At your service, miss!" said Achilles, bowing to her from his perch atop Tortoise.

"Um, hello. My name is Lauren Ipsum." She attempted a curtsey.

"How did you get here, Miss Ipsum?" asked Tortoise.

"I don't really know," Laurie said. "We were following the path to Symbol, but I got turned around at Recursion Junction."

"That often happens. You spent quite a bit of time chasing your tail, I imagine."

"But I don't have a tail," she said.

"So it got away from you, did it?"

"What?" Laurie asked. "No, I don't—"

"Or perhaps it was optimized away," said Tortoise. "No matter. Most of you made it through, and that's the important thing. You can help us resolve a question."

"Well, I can try," Laurie said, not sure that she and Tortoise were having the same conversation.

"Splendid!" said Tortoise. "The question my dear friend Achilles and I are considering is this: how long is an infinite piece of string?"

"An infinite string? Infinite means it's really, really, really, really, really, *really* long. Really," said Laurie. Really.

"Ah! So you agree with *me*," Achilles said. "That means the burden of proof must be borne by the other side."

"The burden of Achilles on my *back* is more than enough!" Tortoise grumbled.

"Friend Tortoise is wise about many things," said Achilles. "But he is clearly wrong this time. He says that an infinite string can be exactly *two inches* long!"

"But how can an infinite string be two inches long?" Laurie asked.

"His claim is preposterous and indiscrete," said Achilles. "We are in continuous disagreement about it."

"I never disagree," said Tortoise. "I only discuss, especially with an intellect such as yours, Achilles. Your understanding has no limit."

"You are too kind, dear Tortoise."

"I mean every word," said Tortoise. "Allow me to suggest a way to settle the question by Experiment."

"Please, suggest away," said Achilles.

"Let us build—hypothetically, of course!—an infinitely long piece of string and then measure it. Miss Ipsum can be our impartial judge."

"I accept. Experiment is always better than mere Theory," Achilles said. "And an impartial judge sounds wonderful, especially when she already agrees with me!"

"Excellent," said Tortoise. "Miss Ipsum, imagine you have an infinite number of pieces of string. If you laid them all end-to-end, would that be infinitely long? Hypothetically?"

"Yes, it must be," said Laurie.

"Infinity is infinity," said Achilles. "It's only logical."

"I wonder. Suppose we start with a piece of string *one* inch long," Tortoise said. "Then add a second piece of string that is *one-half* inch long. How long are they together?"

"One and a half inches," Laurie said.

"And that is shorter than two inches?" Tortoise asked.

"One-half inch shorter. Unmistakably," Achilles said.

"We all agree thus far," said Tortoise. "Perhaps we shall converge upon the same conclusion."

"I doubt that!" said Achilles. Laurie wasn't sure what Tortoise was getting at, but she doubted it, too.

"Achilles, would you please keep count of our hypothetical string? I want to add a third piece *one-quarter* of an inch long," said Tortoise. "Is our string now one and three-quarters inches long?"

Achilles retrieved a much-used notebook from under his helmet and scribbled some figures. "It seems so," he said.

"With one-quarter inch to spare?" asked Tortoise.

"Yes," replied Achilles. "Only one-quarter inch! You are a finger's width away from defeat!"

"Add an *eighth*-inch piece," Tortoise said. "Do I still have some space left over?"

"Yes, but I'll have beaten you soon!" the Greek Logician crowed. "Your string is an eighth of an inch away from the limit, and you've done only *four* pieces!"

"Your arithmetic is correct as always, Achilles. But in the interest of science, let us continue until the bitter end," Tortoise said.

"It won't be long," said Achilles. "What is your next move?"

"I would like to add another piece of string, this time one-sixteenth inch long."

"Done!" Achilles scribbled away. "Only one-sixteenth inch left, old friend!"

"Only that much?" said Tortoise. "Then for the next one, I would like to add a piece of string one thirty-second inch long."

"As you wish, poor Tortoise. One thirty-second of an inch added. There is only one thirty-second inch remaining, and an infinity of strings to go! There will be *plenty* of rope left to trip yourself with!" said Achilles.

"Please add a sixty-fourth-inch piece of string," said Tortoise, "then a one-hundred-twenty-eighth-inch piece, and a two-hundred-and-fifty-sixth-inch piece, and then a five-hundred-twelfth-inch piece, and then—"

"Slow down, Tortoise! You are going too fast," Achilles said. "And those are very big—no, very *small* numbers." He figured and scribbled for a minute. "There is only a five-hundred-and-twelfth inch remaining. It's too bad we're not splitting *hairs*, or you could have gotten a little farther! Do you give up now?"

"*Oh*. I see!" exclaimed Laurie. "Achilles, Tortoise is right."

"What? Don't change your mind *now* when we are so close to victory!" Achilles cried.

"No, I'm sure Tortoise is right," said Laurie. "Don't you see? Every piece he adds is *half* as long as the one before. That leaves just enough room left over. Even if he adds an infinite number of pieces, the string will *never* reach two inches."

"Well, hardly ever," said Tortoise.

Achilles grimaced. "It appears you've proven the impossible again, Tortoise. But just to make sure, I will check the arithmetic *myself*." He continued to scribble in his notebook:

+ 1/512 inch

  + 1/1,024 inch

    + 1/2,048 inch

      + 1/4,096 inch

        + 1/8,192 inch

          + 1/16,384 inch

            + 1/32,768 inch

              + 1/65,536 inch

                + 1/131,072 inch

                  + 1/262,144 inch . . .

"*That* should keep him busy. If anyone has the patience to actually count to infinity, it's Achilles. Thank you for your assistance, Miss Ipsum."

"You're welcome, Mister Tortoise," said Laurie. "I didn't know something so big could be so small."

"That's the Power of Two," said Tortoise. "If you cut a number into two halves, then cut it in two again, and so on, very soon it will be too small to see. But there will always be something left over."

"Mister Tortoise, do you know how long this road is? It feels like it goes on forever. I'm trying to get to Symbol."

"This road is quite long," he replied. "In fact, it is infinite."

"Oh, no! How do I get to the end?"

"You can do it in two simple steps."

"How?"

"How do you think? A step with your right foot, then a step with your left foot," said Tortoise. "Your point of view is what's important. It's integral."

Of course! If an infinite string could be less than two inches long, then an infinite road could certainly be less than two steps, if you looked at it in the right way. Laurie closed her eyes and took a deep breath. She tried to imagine an infinite road. That was a little too much to handle, so instead she imagined a really, really, really, really long road. Then she imagined folding it in half. Then she folded it in half again, and again, and again, and again . . .

When Laurie opened her eyes, Achilles and Tortoise were gone. The infinite road was a tiny, short thing now, hardly more than a stepping stone. She stepped forward with her right foot. Then she stepped again with her left foot. In front of her was a road sign that read . . .

CHAPTER 5

Welcome to Symbol

The town of Symbol was surrounded by high, perfectly smooth walls. A large stream split into two and flowed around either side of the town.

"Do you know anything about this place?" Laurie asked.

"The people are kind of strange," said Xor.

"What does that mean?"

"You'll see."

The path led to a gateway with a turnstile. It looked like this: ⊧

Two boys about Laurie's age were guarding the gateway. One wore a bright white suit and a black shirt. The other had a bright black suit and a white shirt.

Maybe they'll ask me a riddle, Laurie thought. *Or I'll need to figure out which one is a liar and which one tells the truth!* Laurie had read a lot of fairy tales, you see. She believed she was figuring out how this place worked.

"Name?" asked one.

"Laurie Ipsum."

"Password?" asked the other.

"Why, I don't know the password," Laurie said.

"Then you may not enter!" the boys said in unison.

"That's not much of a riddle."

"A riddle? Ha ha, no, begging your pardon, miss. That's not how it works. There are no riddles, no bets, no liars, and no truth-tellers. We've read those books too, haven't we, Tollens?"

"Yes, we have, Ponens. There's none of that mythic fairy-tale stuff in our System, miss. Word games and clever riddles, ha! That's just bad security!"

"But that's not fair!" cried Laurie. "How do I get inside?"

"It's very simple," said Ponens. "If you have a password, then that means you can pass through the semantic turnstile."

"If you can't pass through the turnstile, then that means you don't have a password. It's only logical," Tollens said. "Do you have a password?"

"No, I don't know what it is," Laurie said.

"Then you may not enter!" they said again, together.

"Can you give me a hint?" Laurie was sure she could guess the password, given some kind of clue.

"Yes, hints are part of the System," said Ponens.

"Oh, good."

"Did you set up a hint with your account?" asked Tollens.

"Well, no," she said. "This is my first time here."

"Then it's hard luck for you, miss," said Ponens. "Once you are inside, do make sure to set up a hint for the next time."

"And remember to change your password to something memorable, but hard to guess," said Tollens. "It's just good security."

"But I'm trying to *get* inside! I don't know what to do!"

"It's very simple," said Ponens. "If you have a password, then that means you can pass through the semantic turnstile."

"And if you can't pass through the turnstile, then that means you don't have a password. It's only logical," Tollens said.

"That's not completely true, is it?" Laurie said. "What if the turnstile is broken? I wouldn't be able to enter even if I had a password."

"Um . . . " Tollens looked a little unsure of himself.

"Or what if I fooled you into *believing* I had the password, even if I didn't? Then I could enter without it."

"Hmm." Ponens considered Laurie's argument, trying to find a flaw.

Laurie rushed on. "Or what if I had the password, but I didn't want to give it to you?"

"No, you still couldn't encroach on our premises," Ponens said with more confidence. "You have to give us a password that matches the name you give us."

"Is it 'Laurie'?" she guessed.

"No!" they shouted together.

"Is it 'November First'?" That was Laurie's birthday.

"No!" they shouted again.

"Only one try left, miss," said Tollens.

"Oh, no! Really?"

"You can try only so many times. It's just good security."

"Do I even have an account?" she wondered.

"We can't confirm or deny that," answered Ponens. "That would be bad security."

"Do I . . . *not* have an account?"

"We can't deny or confirm that, either!" answered Tollens.

"It's very simple—" began Ponens.

"—yes, yes," Laurie interrupted. "If I have it, I know it, but if I don't, you can't tell me. And you can give me a hint only if I set it up earlier!" This certainly was very good security. *Think, Laurie, think!*

"Okay, let's start over," she said.

"Very well, miss," said Tollens. "Name?"

"I told you, it's Lau—" she stopped herself. "Actually . . . my name is Eponymous Bach."

"Password?" said Ponens.

It couldn't be that simple, could it?

"Bach's Password."

"Welcome!" said Ponens and Tollens, waving her through the turnstile.

Of course Bach would name her password after herself!

CHAPTER 6

A Tinker's Trade

When Laurie and Xor were safely inside the town walls, the little lizard popped his head out of Laurie's pocket.

"See what I mean? Let's hope they don't figure out what you did to get in here," Xor said. "So, why are we here?"

"We're looking for information that could help me get home. Maybe we can find a map or something."

"Oh," said Xor. "I was hoping you were going to say food. Why don't we try this place?"

In front of them was a storefront with a very fancy sign painted on the window:

N. Veterate Tinker
Algorithms *&* Abstractions
BUY * SELL * TRADE

"*Al-go-rith-ms*. That sounds like a kind of fruit."

"Are you *always* hungry, Xor?"

"Time flies like an arrow, and fruit flies like a banana. Let's see if there's a fruit fly problem I can help them solve."

A bell jingled as Laurie opened the door. "Hello, hello!" the shopkeeper said. "And welcome to my shop. I'm Tinker, and you are looking for a finely crafted algorithm, am I right?"

Laurie looked at the items listed on the chalkboard, but they didn't make any sense.

```
FOR SALE            WANTED
Branch & Bound      Riemann
Convex Envelopes    P̶o̶i̶n̶c̶a̶r̶é̶
Karmarkar's Method  P equals NP
```

"I'm not sure. What *is* an algorithm? Can you eat it?" asked Laurie.

"What? No, it's just a fancy way of saying 'how to do something.' But *Algorithm* looks more impressive on the sign," said Tinker.

Xor turned orange with disappointment.

"How to do something," repeated Laurie. "In that case, I want to find a sensible way to visit every town."

"That sounds like an interesting problem. What have you been doing so far?"

Laurie told Tinker about her adventure in the Red-Black Forest and her visit with Eponymous Bach.

"A Hamiltonian path, eh?" said Tinker. "That's a tough one. I hate to say it, because he sounds like a nice person, but the

Wandering Salesman might take a long, long time to finish his tour of all the towns."

"Oh, no! But why?"

"If you always go to the nearest town you haven't visited yet, you might miss a town that's just a little farther away. Then you go to another town that's closer to you but still farther from the one you missed, and so on. You can end up crisscrossing the whole country to get to the last few towns."

"That sounds exhausting," said Laurie. The Wandering Salesman wasn't so sensible after all! "So how do I find the shortest path?"

"I'll see what I have in stock. But it might be expensive."

"I don't have much money with me," Laurie said. She took a few quarters from her pocket and showed them to Tinker.

He looked at them with surprise. "Quarter Dollar? I don't know what a Dollar is, never mind a quarter of one. Is this money where you come from?"

"Of course it's money! That's seventy-five cents," she said.

"Cents? We use Fair Coins here."

"What's a Fair Coin?"

"Well, they are a bit bigger than those Quarter Dollars of yours, but not nearly as pretty! You can tell genuine Fair Coins because they always flip heads or tails, fifty-fifty."

"But you can flip quarters fifty-fifty, too!"

"That may be true, but I can't just take *your* word for it, can I? Here, all Fair Coins must be certified Fair."

Laurie was crestfallen.

"Don't look so sad! I do want to help you," said Tinker. "Maybe we can do a trade. It so happens I'm in the market for a particular algorithm."

"But I don't have any algorithms, either," said Laurie.

"That's not a problem," said Tinker. "You can compose new ones any time you want, with a little bit of thinking."

"I can? How?"

"Well, everyone develops their own style. You can put little ideas together to make big ideas. Or you put two ideas side by side and compare them. Or you start with big ideas and take them apart."

"You mean like Eponymous does?"

"Yes, just like her. She's a great Composer."

Laurie had never thought that *she* could do things like that herself. But Tinker seemed to think it was normal.

"So what do I do?"

"The algorithm I'm looking for is how to draw a circle," Tinker said. "It's a tough one, so you'll have to use your imagination. I've asked all the adults and even Ponens and Tollens already, but all they do is mutter about x squared plus y squared and never get anywhere."

"Take a look at this." He handed Laurie a wind-up toy animal. It had a Shell, and was Round and Green. "This turtle can do three things: it can move forward or backward, it can turn, and it can draw a little dot on the paper."

"Hey, that's pretty neat!"

"Yes, but the thing is, it doesn't know how to do anything else. That's where the algorithm comes in." Tinker took out a piece of paper and wrote what looked like a little poem:

> Go forward one inch,
> make a mark,
> repeat five times.

Then he wound up the turtle and placed it on the poem. It went *zzzrbt bzzaap whuzzzsh*, and so on. Then it drew a line of dots, just like the poem said:

"You see? If you put little ideas together, you can make bigger ones," Tinker said. "And you can compose *those* ideas into even bigger and bigger ones."

"How do you do that?" asked Laurie.

"By giving them a name. You can use the name like a handle: you'd carry a pot of soup by the handle, and you can move around an entire idea just by writing its name. Here, let's call the first idea *LINE*. Then you can put four lines together to make a square."

```
LINE:
Go forward one inch,
make a mark,
repeat five times.


SQUARE:
make a LINE,
make a right turn,
repeat four times.


make a SQUARE.
```

The little turtle *zzzrbt*ed and *whuzzzsh*ed and *bzzaap*ed, then drew this:

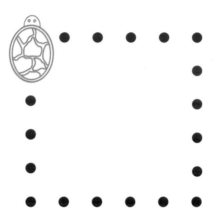

Laurie was amazed. It was like magic, but every step made sense.

"So, knowing what the turtle can do, can you teach it how to draw a circle?" Tinker asked.

"I don't know," Laurie said, "but I want to try!"

"That's good enough for me. Here, you can work at my desk. There's plenty of paper and compasses and things like that."

Laurie sat down at Tinker's desk. She doodled with the compass and played with the turtle for a while, trying to remember what she knew about circles.

A circle is round. No, not just round—perfectly round. You put the pin in the center, and the pencil spins around. To make a bigger one, you open the compass; to make a smaller one, you close the compass. If you change the width of the compass when it's spinning, it doesn't make a circle . . .

Suddenly an idea, or maybe a memory, popped into her head: *a circle is all of the points that are exactly the same distance from the center. Hmm, what if you . . .*

Go forward one inch,
make a mark,
go back one inch,
turn right a tiny bit,
then repeat!

After Laurie wrote out her poem, she wound up the little turtle again and placed it on the paper. It buzzed and burbled for a moment, then drew this:

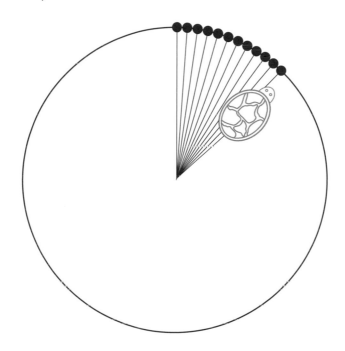

"It's working!" she called to Tinker. "Hey, it's not stopping." The turtle was drawing over dots it had already drawn.

"I think it's because you told it to repeat, but not how many times," said Tinker.

"Well, it should stop when the circle is done," Laurie said.

"It doesn't really understand circles," Tinker said. "It's just a toy turtle, remember? You have to teach it."

Laurie thought a little more, then rewrote her poem:

CIRCLE:
Go forward one inch,
make a mark,
go back one inch,
turn right one degree,
repeat three hundred sixty times.

Then she realized that she could make circles of any size she wanted. It was just like opening the compass wider.

TWO-CIRCLE:
Go forward two inches,
make a mark,
go back two inches,
turn right one degree,
repeat three hundred sixty times.

"This is interesting. You're working really hard!" Tinker scratched his head. "But as it is, it's no good."

"Why?"

"People want to make lots of different circles," he said. "I'll have to keep a lot of algorithms of different sizes, just in case someone wants three-and-nine-thirteenths inches or four-and-three-quarters inches."

"Well, what if you tell the turtle how big to make the circle?" she said. "Maybe like this."

```
ANY-CIRCLE (how-big?):
Go forward how-big? inches,
make a mark,
go back how-big? inches,
turn right one degree,
repeat three hundred sixty times.
```

"And *then*," she said, "instead of ONE-CIRCLE or TWO-CIRCLE, you can say ANY-CIRCLE(one), or (two), or even (one-and-eleventy-sevenths)!"

"Good idea, Laurie. That's a lot simpler," said Tinker. "I was worried you were going to fill my shop with circles!"

"You know, the turtle is drawing really slowly. Not like when it was drawing the square," she said.

It was true. The turtle would crawl all the way to the edge of the circle, then make a mark, then crawl all the way back to the center, 360 times. With small circles it wasn't too bad, but big circles took a lot longer.

"Hmm," Tinker said. "It spends a *lot* more time running back and forth than it does making marks. Do you think you can reduce the running time?"

It makes sense, but it isn't sensible. Laurie thought and doodled, and doodled and thought, but she couldn't figure out how to make it more sensible. The turtle has to go back to the center, right? How else could it know where the edge of the circle was?

Laurie let her eyes wander around the room. Xor was staring at a moth that was flying in lazy loops around a lightbulb. His skin was slowly fading from red to yellow and back to red. The moth went around and around. It was hypnotic. Around and around and around and . . .

Oh! If the moth doesn't have to go to the center of the lightbulb to fly around it in a circle, then why does the turtle need to go back to the center to draw one?

Laurie reached for a fresh piece of paper before the idea got away. *Don't let a new thing out of your sight without a name.*

```
MOTH-CIRCLE (how-big?):
Go forward how-big? inches,
make a mark,
turn right one degree,
repeat three hundred sixty times.

make a MOTH-CIRCLE (one).
```

The turtle went *bzzaap* and *zzzrbt* and *whuzzzsh* and then it started to draw. It moved one inch, made a dot, then turned a tiny bit, then moved one inch, then made another dot . . .

"Whoops. It's making a *huge* circle! Let me try a small number." Laurie didn't have a small number handy, so she borrowed one she had heard from Tortoise: one thirty-second of an inch.

"That's better," Laurie said.

"Let me see," Tinker said. "Wow, look at the little guy run!"

"That was fun," said Laurie. "I didn't know you could just make up new ways to do things."

"Of course you can. Often you aren't the first to think of something, but if it works, who cares? Now, for my end of the trade."

"Did you find the shortest path?" Laurie asked.

"Not exactly. The bad news is that what you are trying to do is impossible."

"It's impossible?"

"Well, highly improbable. There are many different ways to visit all the towns. It seems like you could write an algorithm for the turtle to try each one and find the shortest, right?"

"Sure, why not?" said Laurie.

"There are twenty-one towns in Userland. How many paths do you think there are?" Tinker said.

"I don't know," said Laurie. "A hundred?"

"Way more."

"Um, a million?" Laurie said.

"More like a million million times that!" said Tinker.

"But how can that be?"

"Let's say there are only three towns: A, B, and C," Tinker said. "You are already standing in A, so you have to worry only about B and C. How many ways can you go?"

"Well," she said, "I could go from B to C, or go to C and then B. That's two."

"That's right! But BC is the same as CB, just backward. Every path has a mirror image, so with three towns there is really only one possible path that visits them all. What if there were four towns, A, B, C, and D?"

Laurie counted on her fingers. "I could go BCD, or BDC, or CBD, or CDB, or DCB, or . . . DBC. Six! No, three."

"That's three times as many. Add another town, and you have twelve times as many," Tinker said. "Add a sixth town and there are *sixty* different paths through all of them. With seven towns there are *three hundred sixty paths*. As you add more towns, the number of paths gets very big!"

3 towns: $2 \div 2 = 1$
4 towns: $2 \times 3 \div 2 = 3$
5 towns: $2 \times 3 \times 4 \div 2 = 12$
6 towns: $2 \times 3 \times 4 \times 5 \div 2 = 60$
7 towns: $2 \times 3 \times 4 \times 5 \times 6 \div 2 = 360$
8 towns: $2 \times 3 \times 4 \times 5 \times 6 \times 7 \div 2 = 2,520$
9 towns: $2 \times 3 \times 4 \times 5 \times 6 \times 7 \times 8 \div 2 = 20,160$

"For twenty-one towns you have to multiply one times two times three times four, all the way up to twenty. It makes a HUGENORMOUS number!"

$$2 \times 3 \times 4 \times 5 \times 6 \times 7 \times 8 \times 9 \times 10 \times 11 \times 12 \times$$
$$13 \times 14 \times 15 \times 16 \times 17 \times 18 \times 19 \times 20 \div 2 =$$

$$1{,}216{,}451{,}004{,}088{,}320{,}000$$

"!" said Laurie.

"Indeed!" Tinker said. "All of that 'one times two times three' stuff takes too long to write. So you can use the exclamation point as a shorthand."

$$20! \div 2 = 1{,}216{,}451{,}004{,}088{,}320{,}000$$

"But that's . . ." Laurie said, counting the commas, "over one million million *million* paths!"

"One of those umpty-million paths is the shortest," Tinker said. "I don't know of any way to find it quickly."

"I'll be old before we check them all! Isn't there a better way to do it?"

"Ah, that's the good news!" Tinker said. "I deal only in Exact answers. But there is a brilliant Composer who lives in Permute, named Hugh Rustic. He deals in Good Enough answers. I send him all of my hardest cases. I'll write an IOU that you can take to him."

CHAPTER 7

Read Me

Laurie and Xor were halfway to Permute when a creature with red skin and horns and a black leather jacket pulled up on a red motorcycle. On the back of the bike was a huge bag full of packages and envelopes.

"Hello, who are you?" Laurie asked.

"I'm a daemon. Who else would I be? Hold on, there's a message for you in here somewhere." He rummaged around in his bag and handed Laurie a plain envelope. When she opened it, all she found inside was the strangest nonsense:

> LOREM IPSUM, ESXIHU! SIT AMET, CONSECTETUR ADIPISICING ELIT, SED DO EIUSMOD TEMPOR INCIDIDUNT UT LABORE ET DOLORE MAGNA ALIQUA. UT ENIM AD MINIM VENIAM, QUIS NOSTRUD EXERCITATION . . .

"Are you sure this is for me?"

"Are you sure you are you?"

"Well . . . yes."

"Then that's for you," said the daemon. "I never make a mistake of identity."

"But how can you be sure?"

"How can you be sure you are you?"

"Because I'm right here!"

"See? It's only logical."

"But I can't *read* it," Laurie said. "What does it say?"

"How old are you, that you can't read?" said the daemon. "That's a real shame."

"But—"

"Did you know that kids in some countries start reading when they are only 12 months old?"

"I *can* read—I just can't read *this*. It's gibberish!"

"That," said the daemon, putting his riding gloves back on, "sounds like a whole lot of Not My Problem."

"But—"

"Do you accept delivery? Or do I have to bounce it?"

"Well, yes, but—"

"Look, Miss Well-Yes-But, I'm a mail delivery daemon. I work for the Colonel. My job is to deliver messages. What the message says is Not My Problem. Good day!" The daemon sped away, his tires spitting dirt and gravel all over her.

"*Ooh!*" Laurie was so mad that she actually stamped her foot. "That little d-d—"

"What is it, Laurie?" asked Xor, who had been napping in her pocket.

"I think it's a message for me," she said. "But I don't understand it at all."

"A secret message!" Xor said, rubbing his little claws together. "It's lucky for you that my mother's half-brother is a Cryptosaurus."

"A what-asaurus?"

"A *Crypto*saurus. We know everything there is to know about secret messages. Let's see what we've got here." Xor crawled onto the message for a closer look. The paper was white, so of course his skin turned black.

"Hmm. This is a hard one. I don't recognize these letters at all."

"Why are you looking at it upside down?" Laurie asked him.

"Of course, well, uh, sometimes you can see patterns in secret messages that way." He turned the right way around.

"Now, um, let's read it through slowly and look for clues. Con-sec-te-tour a-dee-peace-ick-ing el . . . " Xor's skin rippled as he moved across the letters. " . . . dew-is ow-tay . . . "

"Hey, Xor, wait a second." Laurie had noticed something odd. "Back up just a little."

"Like this?"

"Yeah. Now, think really hard about blending in."

"Okay. What do you see?" he said.

"Your skin. I think I can read it."

When Xor was lined up just right, LOREM IPSUM ESXIHU in black on white became LAUREN IPSUM GREETINGS in white on black.

"You are unhiding the message!"

"Really? I mean, see? I told you I could do it."

"You are wonderful, Xor! Can you get closer to the paper?"

"If I were any closer, I'd be behind it!"

Word by word, they unscrambled the message. But even then it didn't make much sense:

LAUREN IPSUM, GREETINGS! WITHOUT A DOUBT, YOU ARE THE MOST INTERESTING VISITOR TO USERLAND IN A LONG TIME. BUT YOU HAVE MANY LABORS AND SETBACKS AHEAD IF YOU KEEP DOING WHAT YOU ARE DOING. REMEMBER, THE MAP IS NOT THE TERRITORY!
YOUR HUMBLE SERVANT,
COLONEL TRAPP

"Labors and setbacks? The map is not the territory? What does that even mean?" Laurie asked.

"I once heard of a king who wanted to make a perfect map of his territory," said Xor.

"Why did he want to do that?"

"Kings always want something silly, like a book about everything or a chariot with no weak parts," he said. "This king decided that he wanted a perfect map as large as his kingdom. That way, the royal cartographers could fit *everything* in, down to the last pebble and flower. It took seven whole years to finish it. But it was a disaster!"

"Why? What happened?" Laurie asked.

"As a map, it didn't work very well. To measure the distance between two places, you had to travel exactly that distance," the lizard explained. "By that time you were already there."

"Where did they even put such a big map?"

"That was the other thing. King Borges had only one kingdom, so there was nowhere to put the map except right where it was. It was a huge bother, what with the map sitting on top of people's houses, and none of the crops could grow. The people finally overthrew the king and tore up the map. They say you can still see huge pieces of paper blowing around in the desert."

CHAPTER 8

More Than One Way to Do It

Permute was a small village not far from Symbol. Hugh Rustic's shop was easy to find. Its sign was even bigger and fancier than Tinker's.

HUGH RUSTIC

Improbable & Impossible Solutions

"Hello, Mister Rustic?" Laurie called as she stepped inside the shop. "Mister Tinker back in Symbol owes me an algorithm, and he said I should talk to you about it."

Rustic was a tall, loud, messy-looking man with a big red beard. He didn't look anything like the elegant Eponymous or the neat and proper Tinker.

He certainly didn't look how Laurie thought a Composer should look! But Tinker had recommended him, so Laurie handed him the IOU.

"I'm, um, trying to find the shortest path through all the towns. Can you help me?"

"Wonderful! Interesting!" Rustic said. "Tinker sent you to the right place, miss. Improbable we can do right away. Impossible, by Tuesday at the latest."

"But if it's impossible—" Laurie began.

"Only improbable," corrected Rustic.

"If it's *improbable*, how do you do it?"

"By shifting your point of view," said Rustic. "Instead of looking for an answer that fits your problem, you imagine an *answer* and look for a problem to fit it."

"But you can't just change the problem, can you?"

"Why, of course you can! Worrying about the problem is a waste of time! What you really want is an answer, right?"

"Maybe, but I don't understand how," Laurie said.

"How do you buy the best tomato?" he said.

"Well, I . . . what?"

"Let's say you're at the market. You want the best, most perfect tomato. But to find the *best* tomato, you'd have to compare them all, right? You'd look at each and every one, turn it around, maybe squeeze it a bit. For every tomato in the whole market."

"No one does that!" said Laurie. "Well, old Mrs. Harris *does* do that. But my mom says she's a little batty. I just pick a good one."

"See? You already know how to do things the Hugh Rustic way. You don't waste your time looking for the *best* tomato when there are plenty that are Good Enough."

"So instead of trying to find the *shortest* path through all of the towns in Userland," Laurie said, "we look for one that's short *enough*?"

"Why not?" asked Rustic. "Out of all the zippity-million paths, I bet there are a whole lot that are pretty short. You need to find only *one* of them, and that's much easier."

Rustic pulled out a large map and placed it on the counter.

"Here is where we are," he said, pointing to Permute, "and this is where you started, am I right? Let's put some pencils here to stand in for Mount Upper Bound, and a little spoon there for Lower Bound Valley." The map also had markers for Bach and Recursion Junction, as well as many other places Laurie hadn't been to yet.

"Now for the fun part," said Rustic. "Let's ask the ants."

"Ask the *ants*? What are you talking about? Ants can't read maps!" Laurie said. At the mention of insects, Xor was suddenly alert.

"Who says they can't? Next you'll try to tell me that turtles can't draw circles," Rustic said.

"So you teach the ants to read maps?"

"Not exactly. Ants are good at finding their way home already. The idea is to get them to work for us." He opened a jar of honey and put a tiny daub of the sweet stuff on each town.

A minute passed. Nothing happened. Then a little ant crawled onto the table. It smelled the honey and zig-zagged its way onto the map. It nibbled from one bit of honey, then wandered around until it walked into another one.

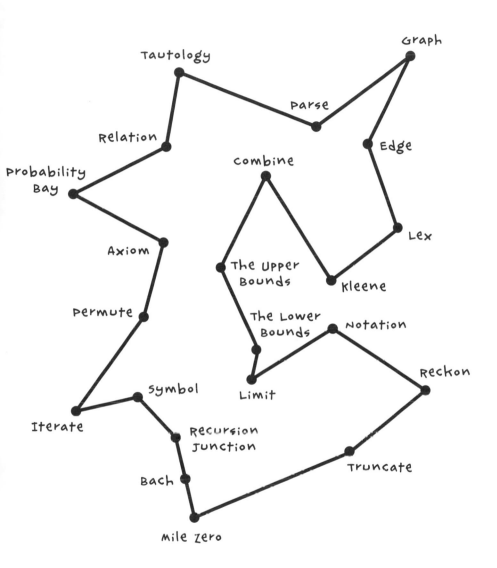

"When an ant finds food, she leaves a little scent message for the others that come after her," Rustic said. "Ants follow the scent of food and also the scent of other ants. Lots of ants can try lots of different paths at the same time. Eventually they'll settle on a quick route to all of the food and back to their nest."

The first ant continued on to Bach. Another appeared and went directly to Recursion Junction instead. Still others went all the way across to Probability Bay, Permute, Notation, and other towns. Soon the map had dozens of ants going every which way, collecting bits of honey and leaving scents for their sisters.

After a few minutes it was clear that some paths were more popular than others. The lines of ants got wider and wider, until there was just one ant superhighway that marched all around the map and back to the nest. Hugh Rustic copied it to a piece of paper before the honey disappeared.

"Ah, there you go!" he said, handing Laurie his sketch.

"Thank you, Mister Rustic! Is this really the shortest way?"

"It's *a* short way. That's as much as I can promise."

CHAPTER 9

Don't Repeat Yourself

Laurie and Xor set out from Permute with their new map. They finally knew where they were, where they were going, *and* how to get there. It was all right there on paper.

"The places on this map have funny names," said Laurie. "*Truncate*. What's that?"

"To Truncate is to make something shorter by cutting off part of it. The town of Truncate has very precise borders," Xor said.

"Oh. So what's *Axiom?*" Laurie asked.

"An Axiom is a rule that you pretend is true even if you don't know why it's true," said Xor.

"Really?"

"Surely. My cousin Nand taught me all about it. She's a Euclidosaurus."

"You're making stuff up again, Xor."

"No, it's just one of those things," the lizard shrugged, turning gray-green. "Either you believe in Axioms or you don't."

"Oh yeah? I bet you don't know what a Furfnoodle is," Laurie said.

"It's a . . . I mean, um. I give up. What is it?"

"A Furfnoodle is a kind of bird," she said. "With long, blue feathers! And it loves eating little lizards."

"Really?" Xor looked worried and checked the sky for blue feathers.

"No. But if I ever see a big, blue bird that loves to eat lizards, I'm going to call it a Furfnoodle."

"You really shouldn't make up words like that," said Xor.

"If you can make up words, so can I," Laurie said.

"I was telling the truth, Laurie."

"It's even fun to say!" she said. "Furfnoodle."

"But—"

"Furfnooooodle!" she sang.

"Look, it's not safe—"

"Furfnoodle. Furfnoodlefurfnoodle. Furf. Nood. Ull!"

There was a *bloop* sound, and a tiny mouse-looking creature appeared on the path in front of them.

"Furfnoodle!" it said in a tiny mouse voice. It ran around them a few times, then zipped off into the weeds, still screaming. *"Furfnoodle! Furfnoodle!"*

"What on Earth was that?!" Laurie said.

"That," said Xor, "was a baby Jargon."

"Where did it come from? It just blooped out of the air."

"You made it with . . . that word."

"I *made* it?"

"I tried to warn you," Xor said. "Where did you think Jargon came from?"

"What's so special about Furf—that word?"

"It's a name that only means something to you. That's what a Jargon *is*," Xor said. "You made it. It's yours."

"But why?"

"No one knows," he said. "It's one of those Axiom things. You have to be careful with names. They have a power all their own."

CHAPTER 10

A Well-Timed Entrance

Probability was a little town on the edge of the sea. It was surrounded only by a rough wooden fence, nothing like the high stone walls of Symbol, and the main entrance seemed to be unguarded. Laurie was walking through the gates, when—

"Excuse me, dear! Hello, on your left." An elderly lady was sitting in the shade just inside. She held a large book on her lap. Her name tag read *Jane Hecate, Border Security*.

"Oh! I didn't see you there," said Laurie.

"That's all right, dear. But before you come in I have to make sure you are on the List."

Laurie had played this game before. "My name is Eponymous Bach, and my password is—"

"Hold on, dear, hold on! One thing at a time. First let's look up your name." She opened the heavy book and started to scan the pages with her finger, letter by letter.

"E . . . E . . . Ah, E! Here we go."

It was painfully slow.

"P . . . P . . . E-P! . . . E-P-O . . . E-P-O . . . no."

Jane closed the book with a thump.

"Sorry, not on the List."

"What?"

"You're not on the List, dear. There are Es, and E-Ps, but there are no names that start with E-P-O. If the *start* of your name isn't on the List, there's no reason to keep looking for the *rest* of it, now is there? It's only logical."

"But her—*my* name must be on the List! She's a great—I mean, I am—" Laurie sputtered.

"Are you a foreigner? I bet your name is spelled differently where you come from. That can happen, especially with foreigners. Why don't we try again?"

Maybe she did have an account after all. "Is it under 'Laurie Ipsum'?"

"Let me see." *Fllliiiip!* "L . . . L . . . L! A . . . U . . . R . . . I . . . Nope. Not here, but I'm sure we'll find it."

"It could be spelled Laur*en* Ipsum."

"L . . . A . . . U . . . R . . . E . . . No, not that way either."

"Uh, Hugh . . . Rustic?"

"H . . . H . . . H! H-U-G-H R-U-S-T-I-C. Ah, *there* you are."

"Great!"

"I'm so glad we could find you!" Jane said. "Your name is spelled quite a few different ways, isn't it?"

"Yeah, I guess it is. Thanks!" Laurie turned to go inside.

Jane held her back with a surprisingly strong grip.

"Your *password*, dear?"

"Oh! Is it 'Rustic'?"

"No."

"Turtle?"

"No."

"Algorithm?"

"A . . . L . . . No."

"Good Enough?"

"No."

Laurie was stumped. "Now what?" she whispered to Xor. "She doesn't care if I try every word in the dictionary. But we'll be here all month!"

"I have an idea," Xor whispered back. "Try 'Abstraction.'"

"What is that? I don't even—"

"My third cousin is a Thesaurus. Trust me!"

"Is it Ab-stract-tion?" Laurie asked Jane.

"A . . . B . . . S . . . No, dear."

"'Trust me,' huh?" Laurie said to Xor.

"Come to think of it, I never liked that cousin."

"Hey . . . did you notice something?"

"Is it dinner time already?" Xor asked hopefully.

"No! When I said 'Turtle,' she said no right away," Laurie said.

"So? It's not the password," Xor said.

"But when I said 'Algorithm,' she took longer to say no. And with Abstraction, she took a little longer than that, moving her finger over the page . . . " Laurie cleared her throat and spoke to Jane. "Is the password, um, About?"

"A . . . B . . . O . . . No."

"See?" she whispered.

"Okay, but what does it mean?"

"Maybe it means the real password starts with AB! So if we keep guessing AB words . . . "

Letter by letter they cracked Rustic's password. It was difficult for Laurie to think of words that started with the right letters. She did not know many of the words Xor told her to try, but he swore they were real, on the honor of Thesauruses everywhere. She knew they were getting warmer because Jane would take longer and longer to say no.

"Abend!"

"A . . . B . . . E . . . No," Jane replied.

"Abdicate!"

"A . . . B . . . D . . . No."

"Abrogate!"

"A . . . B . . . R . . . O . . . No."

"It starts with ABR!" Laurie whispered to Xor. "Abrupt!"

"A . . . B . . . R . . . U . . . No."

"Abraid!"

"A . . . B . . . R . . . A . . . I . . . No."

"We're getting close," Xor said in her ear. "What starts with ABRA?"

"Abracadabra?" Laurie said out loud.

"A-B-R-A-C-A-D-A-B-R-A!" said Jane. "That's the password, right as rain. Welcome to Probability!"

CHAPTER 11

A Fair Exchange

The first thing Laurie tried to do in Probability was buy a muffin, but her strange money wasn't any good. Nobody wanted her "Quarter Dollars." Nobody wanted any algorithms, either.

"Message for you!" A red daemon carrying a mailbag appeared out of nowhere on the street.

"For me?" Laurie said.

"You don't see me talking to anyone else, do you?"

The daemon handed Laurie an envelope and walked away, and once the note was out of the envelope, Xor made short work of the gibberish in Colonel Trapp's latest message. This one was shorter and more useful than the last.

LAURIE, YOU CONTINUE TO SURPRISE ME. I WONDER
IF A BANK CAN HELP WITH YOUR MONEY PROBLEMS.
COL. TRAPP

After reading the Colonel's suggestion, Laurie remembered a building she'd walked past earlier: the Fair Coin Savings & Loan. She rushed back there and stepped inside to find it looked just like banks back home.

"Why are we at a bank?" asked Xor.

"Because I'm getting hungry. It's almost dinner time."

"Finally. But you can't eat money!"

"I can't spend my money either, which means no food. Fair Coins are all anyone takes around here!"

Laurie walked up to the teller window and put everything money-like she had on the counter: a few dollar bills, three quarters, a penny, a dime, and her lucky poker chip.

"Excuse me, sir?"

"Yes?" The teller was a tall, thin man with round glasses. A little card said his name was Trent Escrow.

"I'm from a foreign country and I want to know what these are worth."

"Hmm! I've never seen these coins before! And what are these fancy little pieces of paper supposed to be?"

"That's money, too. One dollar," Laurie said.

"Money made of *paper*," Trent said. "How strange! They are very pretty, but I'm sorry to say they are worthless here."

"Oh no, really? Why?"

"You can't flip a piece of *paper* fifty-fifty, now can you? But these coins are remarkable," he said, examining the poker chip carefully and flipping it a few times.

"Are *they* worth anything?"

"Well, they look pretty balanced to me. But they aren't certified Fair, so no one will take them at face value."

"Tinker said the same thing, but I don't understand," said Laurie. "Where I come from, you can flip quarters fifty-fifty, no problem."

"Ah, but one side might be a *little* different from the other," Trent said, "so it might not be exactly even."

"Really?"

"Surely. The unfairness shows up better if you spin the coin instead of flipping it. That's how we test all of our Fair Coins."

"So my coins are worthless too?"

"Not quite. I can give you an exchange rate: two of your coins for one Fair Coin."

"Why two to one?" she asked.

"Good question!" Trent said. "Most people don't know this, but it's possible to get absolutely Fair flips out of even the most unfair coin."

"I don't believe you."

"Here, let me show you." Trent reached into his drawer and handed her a large, heavy coin. "This is a fake Fair Coin. It looks just like a real one, doesn't it? But it's easy to tell it's fake because it comes up Heads a lot more than Tails."

"So how do you get a fair flip?" Laurie asked.

"Just flip it twice. If you get Heads-Tails, use Heads as your answer. If it comes up Tails-Heads, use Tails as your answer. If you get Heads-Heads or Tails-Tails, just start over."

$$H + T = Heads$$
$$T + H = Tails$$
$$H + H = start\ over$$
$$T + T = start\ over$$

"Oh, I see. The unfairness cancels itself out!"

"Right you are. No matter how unfair a coin is, the odds of getting Heads then Tails will always be *exactly* the same as getting Tails then Heads."

Trent Escrow solemnly exchanged Laurie's five coins and lucky poker chip for three Fair Coins.

"And that's why the rate is two to one."

"Thank you!" Laurie rushed outside to catch the baker before he closed. Dinner!

CHAPTER 12

An Improbable Twist

As Laurie ran out of the bank, a fat policeman grabbed her by the collar. "Got you!" he said. "Why are you running? Did you rob the bank, too?"

"What? Who are you? Let me go!" Laurie yelled.

"I'm Officer Custody, and *you* are in big trouble," the policeman said. "Lauren Ipsum, *if* that is your real name, I arrest you on charges!"

"What charges? What are you talking about?"

"That doesn't matter!" Custody shouted in Laurie's ear, shaking her around. "Charges!"

"Ow! But *what* charges?" Laurie repeated. The officer's hold on her was painful. People on the street were starting to point and stare. If there ever were a time Laurie wished she could disappear like a Steganosaurus, it was now!

"You're going to be difficult? Let's do it nice and proper, if you insist!" Custody took out a roll of paper and cleared his throat.

"Lauren Ipsum, you are hereby under arrest for Attempted Mythology, Counterfeiting Fair Coins, *two* counts of Impersonating a Composer, Hacking in the Third Degree, and Miscellaneous Mopery with Intent to Creep!"

"Let me go! You're the creep!" Laurie tried to twist away, but his grip was too strong. Just then, a shout rang out from the crowd.

"Hey, Custody! Why are you beating up on little girls?"

A tough-looking woman stepped forward to confront the policeman. She wore big boots, black gloves, and an eyepatch in the shape of a heart.

"This isn't a girl, Losesome. This is a dangerous criminal! She broke through our perimeter security," Custody said.

"You mean Jane, that little old lady at the gate?" the woman asked.

"Officer Hecate, yes!"

"Come on, Custody. Jane isn't hard to fool. Last week I told her I was Santa Claus." People in the crowd chuckled.

"That's beside—"

"And what the heck is 'Attempted Mythology'?" the woman interrupted. "I think you just made that up."

"What? I—"

"How do you even know you have the right person?"

"She matches the description!" Custody insisted.

"Really? She doesn't look like Santa Claus to me!"

"No," he said. "She matches the description of the hacker who came through this afternoon!"

"So you are saying a child was able to get through all of your super-duper security?" the woman said, arching an eyebrow skeptically.

"Well—"

"Anyway, this girl is my assistant."

By now Custody was thoroughly confused. "This little . . . she works for *you*?"

"Of course. She's helping me test the security of this place. And if a *child* can run circles around you . . . " She shook her head. "Let's just say, it doesn't look good."

"But you're—"

The woman said nothing. She only smiled, showing a lot of teeth.

Custody was suddenly sweating. He let go of Laurie and pulled out a handkerchief.

"Hey, now, it was an honest mistake! I didn't know she worked for the Col—um, you."

"Well, now you do. And now we're leaving. Come on, Laurel." The woman took Laurie by the arm and walked away, head held high.

"Let's just walk away slowly," the woman whispered. "When we turn the corner, try to make it to the marina before Custody starts using his brain instead of his mouth."

As soon as they were out of Custody's sight, they broke into a run.

"That was great! But my name is Laurie, not Laurel."

"Close enough. I'm Winsome Losesome."

"It's nice to meet you! Thank you for helping me! I didn't mean to cause trouble."

"Don't mention it. I was leaving town anyway. And I really don't like that guy. He's a dumb bully."

At the marina, Winsome jumped aboard a boat and went to work getting it ready to depart. "Come on! Hop on," she called to Laurie.

"Whose boat is this, Winsome?"

"It's my boat, the *Doppelganger*. Get that other rope for me, would you?"

"Wow, how did you get a boat? Are you a pirate?"

"I'm a lot of things, girl." Winsome said. "As for the boat, I kind of stole it. But I stole it honestly!"

"How can you steal something *honestly*?" Laurie was afraid that she was getting into even more trouble.

"I used to be a deckhand on this boat," she said. "The Boss made me do all of the dirty work. 'Losesome, replace the main mast!' he'd say. 'Put a new rigger on the widdershins!'"

Winsome unfurled the sail.

"But secretly, I was saving all the old parts I replaced. They were going to the trash anyway, so might as well keep them, right? Once I collected enough pieces, I quit, and then I put them back together into a boat. Boss never found out, either! The boat he has is all replacement parts. A copy. I have the *real* one."

"But—" Laurie began.

"Think about it later, sweetie? We're busy running from the Law."

Winsome had a point. Laurie untied the rope, and they cast off into the moonless night.

CHAPTER 13

The Game of Life

The *Doppelganger* sailed out of Probability Bay and far away from Laurie's troubles. She risked a peek over the side of the boat and caught a beautiful surprise.

"Winsome! Look at that!"

In the wake of the boat, glowing sparkles lit up the water. Blue and green curlicues danced behind them as the waves fanned out.

"Oh, yeah. Those are called gliders. Pretty, aren't they?"

"They're beautiful! What makes them glow?" Laurie asked.

"When you stir up the water, they glow and form patterns. You can only see them on a dark night like this."

"Wow! I've never seen anything like this!"

"Want to see something *really* cool?" Winsome dipped a shallow pan into the water and set it on a bench. After it settled down, she traced a little figure in the water.

The glowing dots came alive and wiggled around the pan a few times before fading away.

"How do they move like that?" Laurie asked. "Are they really alive?"

"I don't think so. It's just a pattern that looks alive. There are supposed to be some rules about how the glow moves around, but I never paid attention. Maybe you can figure it out."

Winsome went back to minding the ship's wheel. Laurie played with making more gliders, pretty waves, and curls. Xor tried to bite the glowing squiggles as they wriggled by, but all he caught was a mouthful of water.

Laurie got good at finding patterns that skittered through the water for longer and longer, but eventually, she grew restless.

"Winsome, where are we going?"

"We're headed for Abstract Island," Winsome replied. "I have some deliveries to make. We should get there by morning."

"Abstract Island? That isn't on my map," Laurie said.

"I bet a lot of things aren't on your map, girl."

"You mean the map is not the territory?"

"Eh? Who told you that?" Winsome asked.

"Colonel Trapp. He sent me a really strange letter."

"Oh, *him*."

"Do you know Colonel Trapp?"

"He's a crazy old man," Winsome said. "Always messing around in other people's business. Sending those rude daemons with his stupid secret messages."

"The secret messages were fun. Xor figured out how to—"

"Be careful with the Colonel, Laurie. I'm pretty sure he was the one trying to get you thrown in jail."

"Who is he?" Laurie asked.

"He's my—he was my boss," said Winsome. "This was his mail boat. Until I copied it. We . . . disagree about how to do business, so I struck out on my own."

"You had a fight with him?"

"Well, yes," Winsome said.

"What did you fight about?"

"He wants things to stay just the way they are. I . . . don't."

"Oh," said Laurie. Something about Winsome's voice told Laurie not to ask her more about the fight. They were quiet for a time, watching the sky and water.

"The Colonel's right about one thing," Winsome said softly.

"What's that?"

"A map is just a picture. It's not the real thing. If someone forgets to put Abstract Island on a map, the Island still exists. It doesn't care what you know."

"No one in Userland said anything about islands," Laurie said.

"The people back there don't know much about the world outside. That's the way the Colonel likes it. Userland is an island. It's a whole world of islands."

Laurie didn't like what she was hearing. "But Winsome, I have to follow my map to get back home."

"Do you?"

"Yes!"

"Why?"

"That's what everyone told me to do," Laurie said.

"That's not a good enough reason," Winsome said.

"It isn't?" People told Laurie what to do all the time. She didn't always do what they said, of course, but she usually felt bad about it.

"No! You should always know *why* you are doing something," said Winsome, "and not just because someone told you to do it. Keep your head on and be flexible, girl. Otherwise, you're like those little gliders, going wherever people send you."

"But Tinker said—"

"Forget Tinker for a minute," Winsome said. "How did you get lost in the first place?"

"I had a fight with my mom," Laurie said. "Mom wants me to go to school over the summer, but I don't even need to!"

"Maybe summer school is a good thing. I heard that kids in other countries—"

"I don't care! I don't want to waste the whole summer in school with people I don't even know!"

"Okay, that's fair. So then what happened?"

"I took a walk in the woods to calm down a little, but I was so mad that I forgot to watch where I was going, and I got lost, and I spent a long time walking in circles," said Laurie, her eyes filling with tears. "Then I was attacked by those Jargon things, and I ran and ran until I came here, but then I made a Jargon myself because I didn't know the rules, and no one here has even heard of Hamilton, or dollars, or anything! And I don't understand why I need a password, and now I'm going to an island that's not even on the map and—"

"Hey, slow down—" Winsome said.

"—now I'm lost all over again and . . . and . . . " Laurie started sobbing.

"Wait, don't, oh man . . . "

Winsome knew how to handle the nastiest people you'd never want to meet, but a crying girl was something else. She gave Laurie an awkward hug until the noise stopped.

"You done?"

"Yeah." Laurie sniffled.

"Good. I thought you were going to sink the boat," said Winsome. "Why don't you go below and get some rest? And think about something before you fall asleep."

"Think about what?"

"Making your own map."

CHAPTER 14

In the Abstract

"Laurie, wake up."

"Mrfl." Laurie just rolled over. It felt way too early to wake up!

"Come on. Wake up."

"Mom?" Laurie heard water splashing. The bath?

"We're here, girl. Help me tidy up the boat."

"The . . . boat? What b—" she opened her eyes. The walls were made of wood, and it was Winsome, not Laurie's mother, who wanted her to wake up. Of course—Laurie was still on the *Doppelganger*.

Laurie went above deck and got her first look at Abstract Island. The *Doppelganger* was tied up at the end of the main pier. The little harbor was a perfect half-moon. All around the docks, people were fishing or fussing around on identical boats. On land, identical houses and shops were scattered among trees and hilly parks.

"Hey, Winsome, why do all of the buildings look the same?" Laurie asked. "And the trees, too!"

"That's how they do things here. First they talk *endlessly* about what makes a building, or a street, or a pigeon. Once they find the perfect abstract design, they make a bunch of copies. Let's go get some breakfast and then deliver these letters."

Winsome lifted a huge mail bag and headed down the pier. Laurie had to hurry to keep up.

There were many restaurants around the harbor. The Philosopher's Diner was packed with old people wearing togas, and at Random Slice Pizza you never knew what toppings you'd get. It was too early for pizza, though.

They took a booth at the Push & Pop Café and ordered full stacks of pancakes. Instead of cutting through the whole pile of pancakes, Winsome ate them off the top of the stack, one by one.

Mystified, Laurie watched Winsome until she could no longer contain her curiosity. "Why are you eating your pancakes funny?"

"I'm not eating them funny. *You're* eating them funny."

Laurie didn't push the question, but instead tried another. "What should I do about my map?" she asked between bites.

"Beats me, girl." Winsome said. "So let's play a game that will help us figure it out."

"What game?"

"It's called Five Whys. It's a game to play when you get stuck."

"How do you play?"

"I ask you a Why question, and you answer, and then I ask you another, until we find the reason you got stuck," Winsome said.

"For example?"

"For example," Winsome began, pausing to swallow her last bite of pancake, "why do you want to follow that map?"

"It's the one Hugh Rustic made for me with his ants," Laurie said. "He found a short-enough path through all of the towns."

"So why did you want to find a short-enough path?"

"Because there are blippity-million paths through Userland, and Tinker didn't know how to find the *shortest* one," Laurie said.

"Why did you ask Tinker for the shortest path?"

"Because Eponymous said that the Wandering Salesman's algorithm—well, she didn't say 'algorithm,' I figured that out later—she said his algorithm wasn't sensible."

"Why did you want to use the Salesman's algorithm?"

"Because that's how *he* finds his way home."

"Why did you think his algorithm made sense for you?"

"Because I . . . " Laurie hadn't thought about it. "I don't know."

"You were lost and scared, and he seemed to know what he was doing, right?" Winsome asked.

"Yeah, I guess so."

"Sweetie, the Wandering Salesman is a *salesman*. He has to visit many places to buy and sell," Winsome said. "And it's his job to convince people."

"Eponymous said that it made sense, though."

"The Salesman's algorithm makes sense for *him*, but maybe not for you. It's tempting to jump on the first answer that comes along. But a lot of the time, it's not the best. That's why you have to keep your head on."

"Why didn't anybody say anything?" Laurie asked.

"Because it's up to you to ask the right questions," Winsome replied. "No one is going to live your life for you, girl."

"But I *asked* everyone how to get home!"

"No, it sounds like you drifted away from your real goal. By the time you got to Rustic, you didn't ask how to find Hamilton. You asked him how to find a short path through all the towns in Userland."

"Wow, you're right." Laurie looked down at her lap. "I feel really stupid now."

"Nah, don't feel bad. Everyone makes that kind of mistake."

"They do?"

"You have no idea," said Winsome. "Algorithms don't just happen in turtles and ants and coins. They also happen inside your head, and those are the hardest to get right."

"I still don't know how I'm going to get home."

"Neither do I. But asking the right question is a good start. And as long as you're here, you might as well be useful." Winsome pointed out the window to a tall white tower on a hill. "Do you see that lighthouse?"

"What about it?"

"Would you like to go up to the top? The view is amazing."

"Well . . . sure! That sounds like fun," Laurie said.

"Great. Take this." Winsome handed her a heavy wooden box. "I need you to deliver it to the lighthouse keeper."

"What is it?"

"It's very expensive. And fragile."

"But—"

"Go on, he's waiting. I'll meet you back at the boat."

Laurie's climb up the hill was exhausting, so she stopped at the base of the lighthouse to rest a moment before checking for a doorbell or someone to let her in. There was no sign of either on the ground floor, so she shouted at the tower.

"Hello! Hello up there! Anyone?"

A voice came floating down. "Yes! Come up! The door is open."

Round and round up the staircase, Laurie huffed and puffed with the unwieldy box, Xor perched on her shoulder. Finally she reached the lighthouse keeper's room at the top of the tower, completely out of breath. The lighthouse keeper had his back to her, scanning the horizon with binoculars.

"Oh, good," he murmured. "Put it down carefully."

Laurie heaved the box onto a bench and took a look around. The room had no walls to speak of; it was made almost entirely of glass. Laurie stood next to the lighthouse keeper to get a better look out the windows. To one side was the wide blue water. She could barely see a bump on the horizon—maybe that was Userland. To the other side, all of Abstract Island was laid out like, well, like a map. On the coast were the port and the *Doppelganger*. Two people in togas were arguing in front of the Philosopher's Diner. From above, the island looked even more neat and organized.

"Wow! You can see everything from here!" Laurie exclaimed.

"Yes." The lighthouse keeper just kept his eyes glued to the scenery outside.

"So . . . that's it?"

"That's it," said the lighthouse keeper. "Oh, er, thank you."

* * *

Walking downhill, without the box, was a lot easier than going up.

"What *was* in that box, anyway?" Laurie wondered out loud on her way back to the *Doppelganger*.

Xor poked his head out of her pocket. "My guess is light-bulbs. Something boring," he chimed in. "Adults are always making a fuss over boring things."

*   *   *

Back at the boat, Winsome was getting ready to sail again.

"Good work, girl. Thanks," she said as Laurie came aboard.

"You're welcome. He didn't talk much."

"That's how some people get, living in a tower all the time," Winsome said. "Other people start to talk a *lot*."

"They do?"

"You'll see. So what are you going to do now?"

"I thought about it," Laurie said. "Userland is just one island. This island is . . . nice, but I asked around, and no one here has heard of Hamilton either."

"Well," said Winsome, "do you want to be my assistant?"

"What do you mean?"

"You're looking for a way home, right? The *Doppelganger* goes just about everywhere. You can help me make deliveries, and you'll be able to look for answers in a lot more places than you could by walking. Or swimming."

"Isn't that the same as you telling me where to go?"

Winsome smiled. "You're getting smarter by the minute. But don't get too smart. Sail with me for a while. I need the help. If you don't like it, I'll drop you off wherever you want. No hard feelings."

Laurie thought a moment, biting her lip. "Okay," she said, "you've got yourself a deal!"

CHAPTER 15

Cleverness When It Counts

Travelling with Winsome on the *Doppelganger* was lots of fun. Laurie got to see so many strange places and people that sometimes she forgot she was trying to find her way back to Hamilton. But her job wasn't easy.

Whenever they arrived at an island, Winsome would take a huge bag of letters into town and deliver them. She would return a few hours later with a new load of letters to take from that island to somewhere else.

Laurie's job was to deliver the "interesting" packages. (Winsome kept using that word. Laurie didn't think it meant what Winsome thought it meant.) "Interesting" customers lived in tall towers in the middle of nowhere, over shaky, scary bridges, on top of high hills, or on the sides of cliffs. The packages were heavy (and fragile . . . and expensive), and the directions for their destinations were often bizarre and incomplete. Just to make it there and back in one piece, Laurie had to be clever about her work.

Unclear directions were bad enough, but this time, the package Laurie was supposed to deliver didn't have a proper address at all. It just said *FIRST, FOLLOW THE BYZANTINE PROCESS*. Winsome had gone off somewhere, so Laurie couldn't even ask her for help.

"What is the Byzantine Process? I don't even know what it looks like. How can I follow it?" she wondered aloud.

"We're on the Island of Byzantium," said Xor, "so the Process must be the name of the main road. Or a river. Or a road beside the river. It's only logical."

"You have no idea, do you, Xor?"

"Sure I do! My stepsister is an Atlasaurus!"

"What's an Atlas . . . never mind. I don't want to know."

Where to begin was no mystery, at least. The entrance to Byzantium was blocked by an enormous stone building. *All Deliveries Enter Here*, a sign read. A long red carpet led inside to a semantic turnstile with two guards, just like in Symbol. The guards seemed to be in the middle of an argument.

" . . . that makes no sense, Anton!"

"It makes perfect sense, Basil. If you only—"

"Excuse me," said Laurie. "I'd like to pass through."

"Sorry, miss. For that, you must have a Pass signed by the Junior Officer of the Watch—" began Anton.

"—and countersigned by the Senior Officer of the Watch," Basil finished.

"Who are they?" she asked.

"We are."

"Oh, good."

"Lieutenant Basil is the Junior Officer of the Watch, and I am the Senior Officer of the Watch—" said Anton.

"—but only on even-numbered days," said Basil. "On odd-numbered days, I'm the Senior Officer and Lieutenant Anton is the Junior."

"What day is it today?"

"That's what we were discussing before you interrupted," Anton said. "Yesterday was the Thirtieth of Pentember. I think we all agree that thirty is an even number, and so I was the Senior Officer."

"That means today is the Zeroth of Hectember," said Basil.

The Zeroth of . . . ? Well, everything has to start somewhere, Laurie thought. "So Anton should be Junior today, and Basil should be Senior, right?"

"It's not as simple as that, miss!" said Anton.

"There is the question of whether zero is even or odd," said Basil.

"Oh." Laurie had never thought of zero that way. Now she was curious. "So which is it? Even or odd?"

"Zero is even!" said Anton. "It evenly divides by two. Zero divided by two is zero."

"That doesn't prove a thing," said Basil. "Zero divided by *any* number is zero. More to the point, if zero is even, then Anton would have two days in a row as Senior Officer, and I won't stand for that!"

"Even more to the point," said Anton, "if zero is odd, then Basil would be Senior both today and tomorrow, the First of Hectember. I won't sit still for *that!*"

"You see, miss, when it comes to important questions, where you stand depends on where you sit," Basil said.

"But—" Laurie started.

"Anyway, you need to have your Pass Approval Request Form approved first."

"My Pass Approval Request Form? I don't understand."

"Oh, we don't have the Passes here, of course," said Basil. "That would be bad security!"

"You have to get your Pass Approval Request approved by General Case. If he says you can pass, then we say you can pass," said Anton.

"He's down the hall to the right," added Basil. "Now see here, Anton: If you add two odd numbers together you get an even, right? And zero plus zero is zero. So if zero is even like you insist, then it must also be odd at the same time . . ."

Laurie walked down an endless hall until she came to a slightly open door marked *General Constantin Case, Office of Perimeter Security*. She knocked lightly and stepped inside the room.

"Hello, Mister General, sir? I'm looking for a Pass to go through the gate."

"Hmm." General Case looked up from his papers for a moment. "And what is your business?"

"I'm delivering a package."

"Hmm. How many fenceposts do I need for 100 feet of fence?"

"Excuse me?"

"*Fenceposts*, child. I want to put a fencepost every 10 feet for 100 feet of fence. How many do I need?"

"Uh, 10?"

"That's what I thought, too," he said, "but we're running short. I suspect the enemy is stealing them."

Laurie had no idea what he was talking about. "I'm sorry to bother you, sir, but about that Pass . . ."

"Take this to General Darius down the hall, in the Office of Logistics," said Case, handing her a blank Pass Approval Request Form. "If he approves it, I'll approve it."

"Thank you!" Laurie said brightly.

"Hmm." He turned back to his fencepost problem, leaving Laurie to find General Darius on her own.

*   *   *

General Damien Darius was also busy with a stack of paperwork. Laurie noticed a large map of a river on his desk; the map was covered in scribbles and arrows.

"General Darius? I need a Pass," said Laurie, handing him the Pass Approval Request Form she'd gotten from Case.

"Are you here about the mandelbroccoli?"

"Uh, mandelbroccoli? No, sir."

"Then you have information regarding the wolf."

"The wolf?"

"Yes, the wolf," said Darius. "One of my men is trying to move a wolf, a goat, and a load of mandelbroccoli across the Concurrent Streams. The boat is only big enough for him and one other thing."

"Can't he take one at a time?" she asked.

"No good. If he takes the wolf and leaves the goat alone with the broccoli, she'll eat it. If he takes the broccoli and leaves the wolf with the goat, the wolf will eat *her*."

"So take the goat first," said Laurie, doing a pantomime in her head. "And then take . . . oh."

"Yes. No matter what he takes next, he has the same problem on the other side." Darius said.

"That's terrible news, but I'm actually asking about a Pass," Laurie replied.

"And I don't have time for civilian chit-chat. Take whatever this is to General Euripides in the Office of Records," Darius said, handing back Laurie's Form. "If he approves it, I'll approve it."

Down the hall Laurie went.

*   *   *

Euripides had his hands full with a problem of his own. People were crowded around huge record books lying on tables in the Office of Records. Some people were trying to read long strings of numbers from the books. Others wanted to *write* new numbers in the books. The readers and writers were thrashing about, getting in each other's way. It looked like a fight could start at any time.

The General was pacing from table to table, listening to complaints and issuing orders. A crowd of people followed him around, shouting over one another, trying to get his attention. It looked like he barely had time to think.

Laurie pushed and struggled and wiggled her way to the front of the crowd.

"Sir? General Euripides? Can you help me?"

"Eh? Oh, another one. Are you a reader or a writer?"

"I'm not a reader or a writer. I need you to approve—" Laurie began, but the General had to go break up an argument.

"Now what was it you wanted? A reader? Which book?" Euripides asked when he came back.

"No, sir. I need—Sir? Hello, sir?"

Euripides was off to another corner of the room. Laurie tried to get his attention again, but the crowd kept shoving her out of the way.

*　*　*

Laurie sat on the floor in the hallway and put her head on her knees, exhausted and confused. Mandelbroccoli, fence-posts, Passes, General This, General That . . . where did it all end? She could still hear the fighting over who got to use what book next.

"Those people are so rude," she grumbled. "Why can't they take turns and share?"

"Maybe nobody taught them how," Xor said. "My cousin Rex never liked to share. Of course, he was forty feet tall and had teeth as long as your arm."

"Somebody should teach them. It's not fair."

"Yeah," Xor said. "Hey, aren't you Somebody?"

"Me?"

"Yeah! I'm pretty sure you are Somebody. Otherwise, you'd be Nobody, and that wouldn't make sense to Anybody."

"But I'm just a kid. No one pays attention to kids."

"So? No one pays attention to me, either," he said.

"But that's what you want, right? To be invisible."

"Oh. Yeah."

"What are we going to do, Xor?"

"I dunno. Think. You're good at that."

"No, I'm not," Laurie muttered.

"Really? Tinker thought you are. Winsome does, too."

Laurie put her head down again and sighed. "I'm just her delivery girl."

"No, you're her *interesting* delivery girl," Xor said.

"So?"

"So you figure out how to go where other people can't. Remember when you were arguing with Ponens and Tollens outside of Symbol? I didn't think you'd find a way past them. But you did. Same with that scary old lady Jane."

"They never caught us, either," Laurie smiled a little.

"Not until Custody grabbed you."

"And that's when Winsome saved—oh."

"What?"

"I can't go back and tell Winsome that I couldn't even get past the front door!"

"Why not?" Xor asked.

"I just . . . I can't. She gave me a job, and I have to do it myself."

So with nothing else she could do, and nowhere else she could go, Laurie started to think.

She needed an Approval from Euripides so she could get one from Darius. Then, she needed to use *that* to get an Approval from General Case, and finally, the Form had to be signed and countersigned by Basil and Anton. There was something familiar about this Byzantine chaos. Something Hugh Rustic had told her. *Think of an answer, and then look for a problem that fits.*

Euripides was up to his ears with problems. Everyone wanted to do everything at once. Maybe she should start there . . .

* * *

A half-hour later, Laurie was back in the Office of Records. She didn't shout, or shove, or cut in front of anyone. She waited. Eventually one of the books became completely free. Laurie walked over to it and drew a line on the floor.

A woman came over to write in the book. Laurie stepped aside and let her work. A few moments later, a man came up to read from the book.

"New policy, sir," said Laurie. "You have to stand on the line until the first customer is finished."

"But I have to look up something on page 1728!"

"I'm sorry," she said. "General's Orders. But you're next."

"Oh. All right, then." The man stood carefully on the line. Another person came to read from page 1024.

"General's Orders," said 1728, pointing to the line. "Don't worry. You're right after me."

Laurie held the line until the pattern looked like it would keep going on its own. Each new person would be told to wait by the others already in line. Then she waited for the next book to open up.

As the idea spread, people started drawing lines of their own in front of other books. Soon the whole Records Office was calm and organized. After all, it was General's Orders.

Euripides almost couldn't believe what he was seeing. The readers and writers were following a simple rule and taking turns! He was glad to have a rest, and he signed Laurie's Pass without a second thought.

* * *

"General Darius?"

"You again. I don't want to hear about anything else until we've sorted out the Broccoli Situation."

"I think the mandelbroccoli doesn't matter, sir," said Laurie.

"What? You want the goat to eat it all?"

"No, I mean the answer is the same even if you had two wolves instead. You can't leave the goat alone with anything. If you change your point of view, it's easy. I think."

"Go on," said the General.

Laurie thought a little more, then wrote down her idea. It looked a bit like the algorithms back at Tinker's:

1. Take the goat over to the other side.
2. Come back empty.
3. Take the wolf over, but then <u>bring back the goat</u>.
4. Leave the goat and take the mandelbroccoli over.
5. Come back empty.
6. And finally, take the goat over again!

Darius studied Laurie's idea for a while, his hands moving this way and that as he thought it through.

"I believe this will work. The goat won't like going back and forth so much, but it's better than getting eaten," said Darius. "Now what is it you wanted, miss?"

* * *

At last, Laurie arrived back at the Office of Perimeter Security. "General Case, sir? General Darius signed my Pass."

"Hmm," Case hmmed, scribbling a signature below Darius's.

"Thank you, sir."

"Hmm."

"Sir? One more thing," Laurie said.

"Hmm?"

"I don't think anyone is stealing your fenceposts. It's just that you need *eleven* posts. Like this."

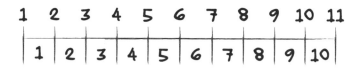

"Hmm!"

* * *

"Welcome back, miss," said Anton. Laurie handed over the paperwork she'd collected from the Byzantine Generals.

"It looks like everything is in order," said Basil, examining the list of signatures. "These approvals go all the way to the top!"

"Have you anything to declare, miss?" asked Anton.

"Declare?"

"What Lieutenant Anton means is," said Basil, "is there anything we should know about?"

"Oh. Well, I think Anton is right. Zero is even."

"No!" said Basil.

"Yes. Zero can't be odd because one is odd, and you can't have two odd numbers in a row, right?"

"Right!" said Anton.

"I suppose not," Basil grumped. "But that doesn't prove it's even."

"Well, if you add an odd number and an even number together, you always get an odd number," said Laurie.

"Um," Basil ummed, thinking about it. "One plus two is three, two plus three is five . . . yes."

"So I can prove whether zero is even or odd. Add it to an odd number and see what you get. Zero plus one is one, and one is odd. So zero must be even," said Laurie.

"I'm still not convinced," said Basil.

"Okay," Laurie said. "If you add two *even* numbers together, you always get an even number, right? Zero plus two is two, which is even. Zero is even again!"

"Exactly!" Anton said.

"Hrmph," Basil hrmphed. "So zero is even. How do I keep Anton from being Senior two days in a row?"

"That's the easy part," Laurie said. "The problem is that yesterday, the Thirtieth, and today, the Zeroth, are both even. Anton was the Senior yesterday. So Basil, you can be the Senior Officer of the Watch today."

"Now hang on a minute—" said Anton.

"—but only until lunchtime," said Laurie. "After lunch today, Anton is Senior. That way it's fair."

"Brilliant!" said Senior Officer Basil. "Junior Officer Anton, sign this young lady's Pass!"

Approved, approved, approved, signed, and countersigned. Laurie was finally through the turnstile.

"I'm glad that's over," said Xor. "Now, where the heck is that Byzantine Process?"

CHAPTER 16

A Change of Plan

SECOND, the package's directions read, *DELIVER TO BRUTO FUERZA, LOOKOUT HILL LIGHTHOUSE.* Laurie and Xor couldn't see any lighthouse, but there was a cloud of dust rising from the hill.

"You work for Winsome, eh? Right on time," said Bruto when they arrived. "I'm sorry to say we're behind schedule. Our lighthouse isn't finished. We've been working double-time, day and night."

"Are you going to put the lighthouse on top of that castle?" Laurie asked.

"Castle?" asked Bruto. "That *is* the lighthouse."

Dozens of Green-Shelled Round machines were busy all around the enormous structure. They looked just like Tinker's turtle, but they were the size of a large truck. Instead of drawing dots on paper, these turtles were laying bricks on top of bricks, making WALLs, STAIRs, and WINDOWs right before Laurie's eyes.

"What are all those things coming out from the wall?" she asked, pointing to a forest of supports and buttresses on one side of the tower.

"We've had no end of problems," said Bruto, shaking his head and spitting. "The south wall was falling outward. So we had to shore it up. Then it started falling *inward*."

"Is that why you're behind schedule?" she asked. There was something about the scene that bothered Laurie, but she couldn't put her finger on it. It looked . . . messy.

"Things are always going wrong," Bruto said. "Big ideas come with big risks. But we can fix any problem with more power and hard work!"

"You certainly have a lot of both," Laurie said, with just a teensy tiny bit of envy. The things she could do with all those turtles! "How do you teach the turtles to build a tower?"

"Here, let me show you." Bruto led her to a tent nearby. A small army of people was working around a table. "First we write the plans on paper."

BRICK-LINE:
Lay a brick,
move forward,
lay a brick,
move forward,
lay a brick,
move forward,
. . .

"That part makes a LINE of bricks. We stack a bunch of BRICK-LINES on top of each other, and that's how a wall gets built. To make the wall thicker, we just add more commands."

```
BRICK-LINE-VERSION-TWO:
Lay a brick,
lay a brick,
move forward,
lay a brick,
lay a brick,
move forward,
lay a brick,
lay a brick,
move forward,
lay a brick,
lay a brick,

. . .
```

"Wow, it just goes on and on and on," said Laurie, flipping through the pages. "It must have taken forever to write all of this."

"Big buildings need big plans. Big plans need big teams. It's only logical," Bruto said. "Writing the plans wasn't the worst part, though. We're running out of bricks!"

"Really? But why?"

"The first version wasn't strong enough, and it fell down. So now I'm making a tower twice as big, twice as thick, and twice as tall. Two times two times two is eight."

"So it needs eight times as many bricks?" Laurie asked.

"It's just a matter of supplies."

"How do you know this version of the plan will work?"

"We're not a bunch of amateurs, girlie. We do extensive testing of our algorithms," Bruto said. "Take a look at this!" Off to the side was a table covered with tiny turtles and tiny bricks.

"Hey, they're building a tower, too!" Laurie exclaimed. Sure enough, the turtles were following the same plan as their bigger cousins.

"We test new plans by building a scale model," Bruto explained.

"But, Bruto, the model doesn't have the same extra stuff keeping the walls from falling down."

"Some problems only show up in the full size. When that happens, we have to adapt."

"Oh," Laurie said. "But if the model is not the same as the real thing, how can you be sure that—"

CRACK!

They turned around just in time to see the full-size tower collapse into a big pile of bricks. Bruto stood still for a long time, watching the dust settle as the turtles got to work cleaning up the mess.

"Are you going to make it even bigger now?" Laurie asked.

"No. What we need . . . what we need . . . is a radical change of plan! All right, everyone," Bruto said to no one in particular. "Clear the decks! Empty your minds! Brainstorm! I want new ideas!"

"*Let's make the walls four times as thick, but the tower only three times as high,*" said one worker.

"*More supports inside and out!*" shouted another.

"*Use bigger bricks!*"

"*Make bricks out of steel!*"

"*Steel is too expensive. How about iron?*"

"*Are you crazy? Iron will rust!*"

"*I told you we should have used a triangle.*"

"*Make the outside steel, but the inside brick.*"

"Good! This is good! Keep them coming. We're thinking outside the box. Anyone else?" Bruto asked.

"Why not a circle, like the lighthouse on Abstract Island?" Laurie suggested. She thought about it for a minute, then wrote out a pair of little poems.

BRICK–CIRCLE:

Lay a brick,

turn right one degree,

move forward,

repeat three hundred sixty times.

TOWER–CIRCLE (how–high?):

make a BRICK–CIRCLE,

repeat how–high? times.

"See? You make a circle of bricks, then put a circle on top of that, all the way to the top!" Laurie explained.

"Ha ha ha, cute idea, girlie! But that can't possibly work," Bruto replied.

"Why not?" Laurie asked.

"It's too small!" Bruto said. "How do you expect to make a great big tower out of a teeny little plan like this?"

"I don't know," Laurie said. It seemed sensible to her, but maybe they knew something she didn't. They were professionals, after all. "I . . . I think it will work."

"Hmph," Bruto hmphed. "Even if it were big enough, it has a major flaw."

"What flaw?"

"Our first plan was a hollow square, and it fell down," Bruto said. "The second plan was a hollow square, twice as big, and it also fell down. Your plan is a hollow circle."

"I don't understand. Shouldn't a circle be stronger?"

"Obviously, the problem isn't shape or size—the problem is that they are *hollow inside!*" said Bruto. "We need to fill up the insides with brick, too. It's only logical."

"*You're right, Bruto!*" said one worker.

"*That's why you're the boss,*" said another.

"But I've seen hollow towers," said Laurie. "They've been built before."

"How do you know they won't fall down eventually? The evidence is very clear," said Bruto.

"*Yes, very clear,*" the other workers agreed, nodding to each other.

"But I—"

"No, I've made up my mind," Bruto said. "The tower must be solid. In fact," he said, looking at the pile, "we're going to build a pyramid."

"A pyramid?!"

"A pyramid can't fall down. It's already fallen down," explained Bruto. "It's one of the perfect solids!"

"*Yes, that's right!*" agreed one worker.

"*Genius!*"

"It's just a matter of more work and more materials."

"Okay! We have a plan," said Bruto. "Everyone, let's get to work! Send Winsome my apologies, girlie, and tell her that we need more time to get it right."

Some people can't be argued with. As Laurie and Xor set out for the *Doppelganger*, Bruto and his team were busy writing out the instructions for his PYRAMID, brick by brick by brick.

CHAPTER 17

Chasing Elegants

"Right," said Winsome, ticking off Fuerza's package on her list. "Elegant Island is next. Now where's that special package?"

"Wow, what kind of animals are those?" Laurie asked. Along the shore, little gray animals with long gray trunks were playing with each other and napping in the sun.

"Those are the Elegants. The island is full of them," Winsome replied.

"They're so small and graceful! It's like they're dancing."

"Yeah. Package, package . . . " Winsome muttered to herself. "Don't they have Elegants where you come from?"

"No. We have ele*ph*ants, but they are all big and clumsy. Are Elegants friendly?"

"Only as much as they need to be," Winsome said. "Found it! Okay, this package is for Fresnel Goodglass."

"The address just says *UNDER THE RED BALLOON*," said Laurie. "I guess that means he's over there." She pointed to a red globe floating above the trees.

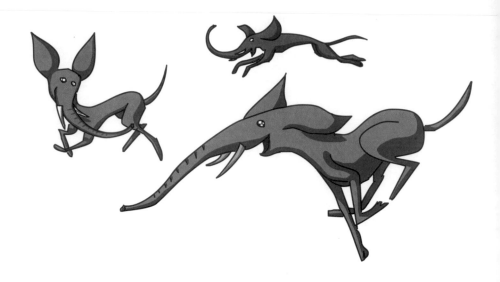

But before she left, Laurie wanted to play with the Elegants. She approached them carefully, making soft "coo, coo" noises.

"Are you a bird now?" Xor snarked.

"Shush. I'm just trying to get their attention."

The Elegants didn't seem especially scared or curious. In fact, they acted as though Laurie weren't there. But their dancing always seemed to take them out of her path. When she walked along the shore, the little creatures drifted inland. When she went inland, they decided that under the trees was the place to be. Soon Laurie could see only a handful of Elegants, playing just outside of her reach. *Oh, well*, she thought.

* * *

With the balloon to guide them, Laurie and Xor found the hill easily enough. But when they arrived, nothing much was there. A large boat anchor was half-buried in the earth. A rope led up, and up, and up to a basket way above the ground, which itself was attached to the balloon. A couple of young Elegants were playing hide-and-seek under the trees. There were no buildings or people at all.

"Are we in the right place?" Laurie wondered aloud. "Where is the lighthouse?"

"Hey, Laurie, take a look at this." Xor was clinging to a sign that read *Please Ring for Service*. A little bell hung below it. They looked at each other and shrugged. Xor gave it a whack with his tail.

DONG-G-G-G-G-G-G-G-G-G-G-G-G-G-G-G

rang the bell, much louder than such a tiny thing should be allowed to.

-G-G-G-G-G-G-G-G-G-G-G-G-G-G-G-G-G-G-G-G-G

Xor was right next to it. The little lizard turned bright indigo and fell to the ground.

-G-G-G-G-G-G-G-G-G-G-G-G-G-G-G-G-G-G-G-G-G

Laurie had to cover her ears until the sound died away.

-G-G-G-G-G-G-G-G-G-G-G-G-G-G-G-G-G-G-G-G-G

When it was all over, the young Elegants were nowhere to be seen. Laurie gathered Xor in her hands. His skin was white and his eyes were rolling around in different directions.

"Xor! Are you okay?"

"I think so. That scared the blue right out of me!"

A hissing sound from overhead made Laurie look up. An elevator box was lowering itself to the ground in front of them. They flinched as the door opened with a polite *ding!*

Laurie picked up her package and, with a last look around, stepped inside. The door closed, and the elevator rose fast enough to make her toes crinkle and her stomach go roly-poly.

When the door opened again, they were a hundred yards up in the air, inside the basket. It was like a little apartment. There was a desk, a bed, and some cozy chairs. A wrinkly-faced old man with a gray beard and pointy ears was smiling at her.

"Is this . . . are you Fresnel Goodglass? I'm Laurie. I have a package for you."

"Yes, it is! Yes, I am! Yes, you are! And thank you!" the man said, taking the package. "Welcome to my Floating Lighthouse. What do you think?"

"This isn't a *lighthouse*," Laurie said, testing the woven floor with her foot before getting off the elevator. "It's a balloon!"

"Sure, it's a lighthouse. In balloon form. See the big light up there?" Fresnel asked. There was indeed a big lighthouse light hanging over them.

"But where's the long twisty staircase?" Laurie asked.

"There is the elevator instead. Easier for my old bones."

"What about the lighthouse keeper's room?"

"You can just look over the side of the basket."

"And the tower?"

"Don't need it! Inessential!" Fresnel said. "The essential part of a lighthouse is the *light*, not the house."

Laurie wasn't convinced. "You can't just stick a light on a balloon and call it a lighthouse."

"I can't?"

"No!"

"Why not?"

"Because . . . it's cheating," she said.

"Hmm. I think I see your point," Fresnel agreed. "But as long as it works, the name doesn't matter."

"Yes, it does!"

"Maybe you're right," he agreed again. "But I am a terrible host! You must be thirsty after all that walking. Would you like some water?" Fresnel offered her a pitcher and glassware on a tray.

"Oh yes, please." Laurie took a cup and tried to fill it. The water splashed onto her shoes.

"*Hey!* This cup has no bottom!"

"That's not a cup, dear child. It's a glass," he said.

"This *glass* has no bottom. How am I supposed to drink out of it?"

"On second thought, that's not properly a glass," said Fresnel. "It's a mug. See the handle?"

"Okay, this *mug* has—"

"On third thought," he said, stroking his beard, "it's made of glass, but also has a handle. So perhaps we should call it a glass-mug, or a mug-glass . . ."

"I don't care what you *call* it!" Laurie yelled. "It's *got no bottom* and the water . . . I mean, um, you called it a glass, but it doesn't have . . . oh." She turned bright red.

Fresnel handed Laurie another mug-glass-cup. "You're right again. Things are what they are, no matter what names people give them."

"But aren't names important?" Laurie asked, checking her new glass-cup-mug carefully for holes. Luckily, this one had a bottom.

"Names go only so far. And many names are actually the same thing in disguise."

"Really?"

"Surely. Are you Laurie or Lauren?"

"Well, both. But I like Laurie. When Mom is really mad, she calls me Lauren." She put her hands on her hips and threw her head back. *"Lauren Ipsum, come downstairs NOW!"*

Fresnel laughed like a horse would laugh, if the horse had heard the joke. "A full name is a powerful thing. But you're the same person either way. And sometimes different things have the same name. You call your mom 'Mom,' but I call my mom 'Mom,' too."

"But I wouldn't call *your* mom 'Mom'!" said Laurie. *How weird would that be?*

"There you go. It's only logical. You have to look *past* the name to see things as they really are. That's Fresnel's First Law."

"You sound just like Eponymous Bach," Laurie said.

"Really? Well, I'm a Composer too," said Fresnel. "I start with big ideas and make them smaller."

"Make them smaller? Why?"

"Why not? Only people with small minds think Big Problems need Big Ideas."

Laurie wasn't sure what he was talking about. "How do you make an idea smaller?"

"By *De*composing. How would you talk about a lighthouse without using the word *lighthouse*?"

"Well, it's a tall white tower near the sea, with a room full of windows at the top, and a big light on top of that, and a long twisty staircase inside."

"That's very good," Fresnel said. "Now look at each part and see if it's essential. If your tall-tower-by-the-sea-with-windows-and-big-light-and-staircase were *pink*, would it work just the same?"

"I guess so. I've never seen a pink lighthouse," she said.

"Neither have I! But if everything already existed, life would be pretty boring. Why is your lighthouse tall?"

"So boats can see you," said Laurie. "A short lighthouse wouldn't work so well. And you need the twisty staircase to get to the top."

"Why the light?"

"The light is so the boats can see you at night."

"And the lighthouse keeper's room?"

"So you can see *them*."

"Ah, so," said Fresnel. "My balloon has a light very high up so people far away can see it. I can look over the side and see them. I get to the top by elevator. The color doesn't matter. It does everything a lighthouse does. Is it a lighthouse?"

"It's *like* a lighthouse," Laurie admitted.

"You drive a hard bargain! I'll settle for 'like a lighthouse,'" he said.

"So that's how you Decompose?"

"That's it, more or less. You take a big idea apart and see the *why* behind each part. Then you look for smaller ideas that do the same thing. For instance, what did you think of my little bell?"

"Your *little* bell! That thing frightened the b—"

"It needs some adjustments, I agree. But the idea is sound," he said. "The essential part of a bell is the sound. Because the bell is way down on the ground, it needs a big sound so I can hear it."

"So why don't you use a big bell, then?" she asked.

"If I used a big bell, I'd need a big frame to hang it from, and a big ringer, and a big sign to go along with it. All the inessentials get bigger," Fresnel said. "There's no need to use a big, complex idea when a small, simple one will do."

"I wish I could tell Bruto that," Laurie said, remembering the giant pyramid. "But he's so far away."

*   *   *

"Winsome, why am I delivering so many telescopes?" Laurie asked.

Winsome's expression turned stony. "It's not nice to open other people's mail."

"I'm sorry. Those packages are really heavy and I wondered what could be so fragile and expensive and important . . ."

Winsome didn't say anything. She pretended to be busy with ropes and anchors.

Laurie pressed on. "Why telescopes?"

"So the lighthouse keepers can see farther out."

"Why do they need to see farther out?"

"Because the other lighthouses are too far away."

"That doesn't make any sense," Laurie said. "Why do people in lighthouses want to see other lighthouses?"

"Because it's how we're going to send messages. It's the Lighthouse Network."

"Why do you want to send messages that way?"

"Right now," said Winsome, "if someone on Abstract Island wants to talk with someone on Data Island, they have to pay the Colonel and his Network of mail daemons."

"Is that a bad thing? Why build your own Network?"

"Because I can. And because Colonel Trapp doesn't want me to."

"Why doesn't he want you to build a Network?" Laurie asked.

"That's Five Whys already, kiddo. Are you ready to go? The next stop is an easy one. You'll like Ping. She lives in a treehouse!"

CHAPTER 18

Many Hands Make Light Work

Once the *Doppelganger* reached the next island, Winsome sent Laurie off on another delivery immediately. This telescope would be the last, but Laurie still wondered how on Earth they fit into Winsome's plan.

"Some things in life you just have to see for yourself!" Winsome said with a smile.

Laurie found it hard to argue with the excitement in Winsome's voice, so she just trusted the usual set of odd directions to lead her to an answer. Before long, she and Xor reached an enormous tree. A long, twisty staircase wrapped around the trunk and up into the leaves, and a young woman stood at the base.

"Hello, Laurie! Glad you made it. My name is Ping Baudot. I've been waiting for you."

"Hello. Wait, how did you know my name?"

"Oh, Fresnel told me all about you."

"Fresnel? He lives way over on Elegant Island!"

"Yes, isn't it wonderful? You and Winsome have been making lots of deliveries lately. The Network is getting quite big now! I can hardly keep up with all the chatter."

"But I don't—"

"You should be very proud. Here, let me help you with that." Ping took the package and raced up the stairs, round and round the trunk of the tree. Laurie followed as best she could.

When they arrived at the treehouse near the top, Laurie gasped in surprise. It was a tree *lighthouse*! Not only that, but the lighthouse keeper's room was filled with telescopes pointing in all directions. A neat label was attached to each one.

"Well? What do you think?" Ping said.

"Why do you need so many telescopes?" Laurie asked.

"See for yourself."

Laurie put an eye to the 'scope labeled ELEGANT. A red, round splotch was hanging in the air. And was that a rope?

"Hey, that's Fresnel's balloon! I can see him! He's waving!" Laurie exclaimed.

Laurie looked into other telescopes. Each one was pointed at a different lighthouse. The one for ABSTRACT showed the lighthouse keeper who didn't say very much, up in his tall white tower by the sea, looking back through a telescope of his own. He didn't wave. The BYZANTIUM telescope showed half a pyramid covered in giant mechanical turtles. Bruto was busy counting bricks.

Ping put down the heavy package Laurie had delivered and released the latches. Inside was a squat telescope. "Excellent! I've been waiting for this."

"It's for the Network, right? Will you show me how it works?" Laurie asked.

"Of course," Ping said. "Watch this." She went to the middle of the room and turned a giant wheel until a red arrow pointed directly at Elegant Island. Then she pulled a lever up and down quickly:

FLOP. FLOP. FLIP. FLOP. FLIP.

FLOP. FLIP. FLIP. FLOP. FLOP.

"Now look at Fresnel again," she said.

Laurie put her eye to the Elegant Island telescope. Fresnel had pointed *his* light at *them* and began blinking a message:

FLOOSH. FLOOSH. FLASH. FLOOSH. FLASH.

FLOOSH. FLASH. FLASH. FLOOSH. FLOOSH.

"He answered back! What did he say?" Laurie asked.

"Oh, he just said 'hi.'"

"All that just for 'hi'?"

"That's how the Baudot Code works," said Ping. "Sentences are made of words, and words are made of letters, right? In the same way, we make *letters* out of FLIPs and FLOPs. Like this."

$$01001 = \text{L}$$
$$11000 = \text{A}$$
$$10011 = \text{U}$$
$$01010 = \text{R}$$
$$01100 = \text{I}$$
$$10000 = \text{E}$$

"That's pretty neat! But I still think it's a lot of work just to say 'hi.'" Laurie said.

"Maybe you're right," Ping said, smiling. "But now that the hard work of building the Network is finished, we can do something *really* interesting: use the Network to make itself better."

"How do you do that?"

"Well, I'm working on a way to use two colors of lights. Fresnel has an idea for a simpler Code that uses only four FLIPs or FLOPs, though I'm not too sure how that will work. We use the old Baudot Code to talk to each other about our ideas for new codes, and then try them out."

"So . . . you can use the Network to talk about how to use the Network?"

"And you helped make it possible, Laurie, by delivering all of those telescopes. Now, the Network will only get better and better as we learn how to use it. We can already pass a message from one end of the Network to the other in just a few minutes! Even the *Doppelganger* takes a couple of days to deliver the mail that far. Everyone will want to use it once we work out the bugs."

"But . . . what about Winsome? Is she going to lose her job?" Laurie asked.

"What? No, not at all! The Network was her idea."

"It was?"

"Sure! All of us work for Winsome. She doesn't want to spend her days hauling mail bags around. That reminds me," Ping said, searching through a pile of paper, "Winsome says she has one more job for you."

"Oh! What is it?" Laurie asked.

"She wants you to deliver this letter to a person on the other side of the Garden of Forking Paths."

There was no name on the envelope, but that wasn't half as strange as some of the assignments Laurie had been given in her time on the *Doppelganger*. If she got it done quickly, she could come back here and play with the Network. "So how do I get to the Garden?"

"You're in a hurry, huh? I'll show you where it is."

CHAPTER 19

Branching Out

The Garden was surrounded by a hedge at least eight feet tall. The entrance was an archway cut out of the bushes. A wooden sign above the entrance read

WELCOME TO THE GARDEN

OF FORKING PATHS.

"Here you go," said Ping.

Laurie was suddenly very worried. "Ping, is this a laba . . . laber . . . one of those garden mazes?" Laurie had read stories about little girls and garden mazes, and they never ended well. Garden mazes were full of monsters and twisty little passages between you and the exit.

"It's not really a labyrinth. You can always find a way out," said Ping. "Where you end up is a different story."

"Oh, good. After I deliver this letter, can I come back to the Treelighthouse? Maybe we can ask the Network about how to find Hamilton!"

"That's . . . a good idea. Yes. When you're done, if you want, we can talk about it."

"Thank you! See you soon!"

"Good-bye, Laurie. Take care of yourself."

Laurie and Xor stepped through the entrance into a kind of hallway made of more bushes. After a short walk, they found a small fountain with a sign above it.

LEAVE A COIN. MAKE A WISH.

Laurie dropped her last Fair Coin into the fountain, closed her eyes, and made a wish. She held her eyes closed for an extra moment just in case. But nothing exciting happened.

She kept walking down the green hallway. There wasn't much to see except hedges, and more hedges, and more signs that talked about the Garden.

DID YOU KNOW?
THERE ARE 16,777,216 PATHS
THROUGH THE GARDEN.

"Only 16 million? That's nothing!" Laurie said. "Userland had millions of millions of *millions*."

ONLY ONE PATH PER VISITOR.

"That's okay. I want to get through here quickly."

ONLY ONE VISITOR PER PATH.

"Isn't that the same thing?"

NO.

"I wonder which path is the shortest," Laurie said. The next sign answered her question.

ALL PATHS ARE THE SAME LENGTH.

"Then how do I know which one to take?" she asked.

CHOOSE WISELY.

That's when she came to the first fork in the path. Each fork had its own sign. The left-hand sign said

👈— THINGS

and the right-hand sign said

IDEAS —👉

Laurie had seen a lot of Ideas lately. A simple Thing would be a nice change. She took the left-hand path. A minute later she came to the next fork. The signs there said

👈— FAMILIAR THINGS | STRANGE THINGS —👉

"I've seen a lot of Strange Things lately, too," she said. "I'll go for Familiar."

⟵ **YOUNG | OLD** ⟶

"Um . . . Old!" Down the right-hand path they went.

⟵ **INTERESTING | BORING** ⟶

"That's an easy one," said Xor. "Interesting."

"You're not the one who has to climb rocks and cross scary bridges when we make Interesting deliveries," Laurie said. "But okay."

⟵ **LOST | UNLOST** ⟶

"How can you have a sign pointing to Lost things? Wouldn't that make them Unlost?" asked Xor.

"Maybe they're only Lost until you find them," Laurie mused.

"That makes sense." Xor replied. They took the left path.

⟵ **MOSTLY LOST | COMPLETELY LOST** ⟶

"Comp . . . no, *Mostly* Lost," Laurie decided. Left again.

"You know, I don't see millions of paths," said Xor. "There's only ever two."

⟵ **SMALL | NOT-SMALL** ⟶

"Not-Small!" they said together.

BIGGER THAN YOU?

🖎— NO | YES —🖝

"Everything is bigger than me," said Xor. "Let's go right."

BIGGER THAN A MOUNTAIN?

🖎— YES | NO —🖝

Not that big! They went right again.

TALLER THAN A LIGHTHOUSE?

🖎— NO | YES —🖝

Lauric had seen quite enough of lighthouses, too. She tried to go left, but a Shelled Green Round animal barred the way.

"We meet again, Miss Ipsum," it said.

"*Mister Tortoise!* What are you doing here?"

"I'm enjoying a special treat," said Tortoise, taking a bite out of the greenery. "I help keep the mandelbroccoli bushes in the Garden nice and trim. For me it is a delicious chore. And what are you doing here, Miss Ipsum?"

"I'm looking for the nearest exit so I can deliver a letter."

Tortoise seemed to smile. Of course, he always seemed to be smiling. "There are millions of paths through the Garden. All of them are exactly the same length."

She tried to picture so many paths side-by-side. "I don't understand. If there are so many, where are they?"

"They are all around you. Every path forks off from another path," Tortoise said. "One path becomes 2, 2 becomes 4, then 8, 16, and so on. After 24 forkings, there are over 16 million different paths."

"Oh! It's the Power of Two again. But this time it gets bigger instead of smaller," Laurie said.

"Exactly right. You are currently on the path to Things that are Familiar, Old, Interesting, Mostly Lost, Bigger Than You, and Smaller Than a Mountain," said Tortoise. "I suppose I am one of them."

"So how do I choose which forks to take?"

"I suggest choosing wisely. Good day, Miss Ipsum." Tortoise turned and walked slowly and steadily down the left-hand path.

"Wait! I don't know what you mean!" Laurie ran after him. Catching up with a Tortoise should have been easy. But with every step he got farther and farther away. By the time Laurie got to the next fork, he was nowhere to be seen.

☜— FRIENDLY | UNFRIENDLY —☞

"What do you think, Xor? Which way?"

"Do you really want to see a Garden full of Unfriendly Things?"

"Good point." She went left.

☜— IN THE AIR | ON THE GROUND —☞

They didn't want to see anything bigger than them that also could fly, no matter how Friendly. Anyway, Tortoise was on the ground.

☜— LIGHT | HEAVY —☞

"Heavy for sure!" shouted Xor.

☜— LIVES OUTSIDE | LIVES INSIDE —☞

"Tortoises live outside, don't they?" Now that she thought about it, Laurie wasn't completely sure. But it seemed like a good guess!

☜— NEVER SLEEPS | SOMETIMES SLEEPS —☞

"And they definitely sleep," said Xor. Right they went.

☜— SLEEPS AT NIGHT | SLEEPS DURING THE DAY —☞

"Sleeps at Night!" Laurie shouted. "We should be getting close!"

☜— MANY COLORS | ONE COLOR —☞

Laurie ran down the left-hand path without stopping to think. But wasn't Tortoise only one color? It was too late to go back.

☜— QUIET | NOISY —☞

"I don't like Noisy Things," she said. "Tortoise is pretty quiet."

☜— PLURAL | SINGULAR —☞

"What does that mean?"

"*Plural* means more than one. *Singular* means only one," Xor said. They went right.

☜— NATIVE | FOREIGN —☞

"I know this one," said Laurie. "*Native* means from here. *Foreign* means from somewhere else. Native!"

☜— EXPECTED | UNEXPECTED —☞

"I wonder where we'll end up," she said as they turned right. "What is Familiar, Old, Interesting, Mostly Lost, Bigger Than Me but Smaller Than a Mountain and Shorter Than a Lighthouse, Friendly, On the Ground, Heavy, Lives Outside, Sleeps at Night—" (she paused to breathe) "—has Many Colors and is Quiet, Singular, Native, *and* Unexpected?"

☜— YOUR WISH | SOMEONE ELSE'S WISH —☞

"MY wish!" said Xor and Laurie at the same time. They giggled and walked down the left path. The next sign made them think for a moment. It asked

ARE YOU SURE?

← YES | NO →

"Sure, I'm sure!" said Laurie. "Why would I ever want someone else's wish?" She went down the left-hand path. "I think we're almost through the Garden, Xor!"

She started walking fast, then jogging, then running again down the long green hallway. Xor was getting excited too, turning all sorts of polka-dot colors. Laurie was already thinking about what messages she wanted to send to Fresnel, and Tinker, and—

"Oh no!"

Laurie stopped dead in her tracks. In front of them was another forking. The last one.

The left-hand sign said

← HAMILTON (LAURIE'S WISH)

And the right-hand sign said

AUNT VANA (XOR'S WISH) →

"The Garden guessed my wish!" Laurie said.

"Mine, too," Xor said.

Laurie started to go left, then stopped. Then she started to go right, but had second thoughts. They stood there for a very long and very silent minute.

"We can only take one path," said the girl.

"Yeah," the lizard replied.

"And there's no going back."

"That's the rule."

"You really want to find your aunt," Laurie said.

"And you really want to go back home," Xor sighed.

"That means we have to choose," Laurie said. "But how?" She did want to go home, but she also wanted Xor to find Aunt Vana. She wanted to bring Xor and Vana home with her and how cool would that be and—

"No, Laurie," Xor said sadly. "It means we have to split up."

"But—"

"Only One Visitor Per Path. That's the rule." He jumped off her shoulder and landed on the right-hand sign. "I guess . . . this is how you found me." His skin turned orange and purple.

"We can do this," said Laurie, thinking furiously. "Once you find your Aunt Vana, take her to the Treelighthouse. I'll find a way to come back. Or maybe I'll get a telescope and a big light and—"

"We'll see each other again," Xor said.

"Okay," said Laurie. "Promise?"

"Promise."

"And I'm going to whistle, okay?"

"Okay."

"So you can hear me."

"Right," said Xor.

"It'll be fine."

"Absolutely," agreed Xor.

"Here I go."

"Me too."

Laurie did try to whistle, but it's impossible to whistle and cry at the same time. Just try it.

CHAPTER 20

Fin

The mandelbroccoli bushes got shorter and wilder until they blended in with the forest. Laurie didn't know where she was or where she was going. But she knew how to get there. At least, she hoped she did. By now it was late afternoon and the shadows were getting longer.

The trees of the forest were large oaks and maple, with an occasional pine or spruce. There were a number of saplings and bushes of various sorts. It was hard to see far because of all the leaves, but walking was easy enough if she skirted the spruce and berry bushes.

"*Chirrrup!*"

Laurie's heart started pounding. More Jargon? How many? Where?

"*Chirrrup!*"

No running this time. She walked toward the noise as quietly as she could. It seemed to be behind a large tree. No, not a Jargon. It was . . . a squirrel. An ordinary squirrel. It yelled what were probably very nasty things in Squirrel, then ran up the tree to safety. And that tree! She recognized it. It was the big tree behind her house, at the edge of the woods . . .

Laurie was home.

* * *

Lying in her own bed after a hot bath made Laurie feel happy and tired. As far as her mother knew, Laurie had been gone only an hour or two. To Laurie, though, it felt like at least a week since she'd gotten lost in the woods. She was too sleepy to think about it. She hoped Xor had gotten his wish and was learning how to blend in. She was sad that she didn't get to see her new friends again. She had promised to come back . . . after delivering . . . delivering that letter . . .

Two seconds later, she was out of bed and tearing open the plain white envelope.

Hi, kiddo. If you're reading this letter, you've figured out who it was for. I wasn't sure the Garden would actually work, and I don't like good-byes.

You helped us build the Network. We couldn't have done it without you. Fresnel says once you learn a few things and unlearn some others, you'll make a good composer.

see you around,
capt. Winsome "Losesome" Trapp

She read it twice before she noticed that Winsome's last name was Trapp. It made sense. For all of the sour things Winsome had said about Colonel Trapp, they were a lot alike, sending strange messages and bossing people around. It looked like Laurie wasn't the only one who had trouble getting along with her parents.

She lay down again and thought about tomorrow. Tomorrow was the first day of summer school. It didn't sound as scary as it did before. If she could navigate the Byzantine Process, beat Ponens and Tollens, make infinite strings, and teach turtles to build towers, sitting in a classroom didn't sound that hard at all.

She might even learn something interesting.

The End

CHAPTER 21

One More Thing

It was a dark and foggy night, many months after Lauren Ipsum had gone back home to Hamilton. A lighthouse flashed. Flashed. Flashed. Flashed.

The flashes didn't carry any messages this night. The fog was too thick to send signals, so the Network was down. The powerful lights were needed for their original purpose: to warn boats away from dangerous rocks.

As it happened, only one boat was around, and it didn't need warning. It was exactly where it was supposed to be.

The *Jargonaut* was the boat, and Kevin Kelvin was its captain. The boat was large and flat and plain. Near the front was a little cabin where Kelvin lived. The rest of the deck was taken up by a crane and a winch—a machine built to wind wire in or out. A wire led from the crane and into the water, looking like a large fishing pole. Belowdecks was mostly a hold for tons and tons of coiled wire.

It wouldn't be accurate to say that the *Jargonaut* was a gigantic boat with a winch attached to it. That might give you the wrong impression. It would be better to describe it as a gigantic *winch* with a boat attached to it. Its entire purpose in life was to play out and wind up miles of heavy wire.

Inside the cabin, Kevin Kelvin rubbed his hands together to keep them warm. A thermometer hung from a peg near the door. It read a chilly 273. *Brrrrr!*

Now, 273 degrees might sound pretty hot to you and me, but this thermometer didn't measure in degrees Fahrenheit or Celsius. It was on the Kelvin Scale, one of the captain's many inventions. The Kelvin Scale starts at Absolute Zero, the coldest that any cold thing can possibly get. And 273 Kelvin isn't much better. It's about the temperature of an ice cube. *Brrrrr!*

The thermometer said a lot about the kind of person Kevin Kelvin was. He was a Composer, and a wickedly smart one. He never let a good idea escape without putting his name on it.

When people asked Kelvin what he was doing, he would say he was fishing. He never explained what he was fishing *for*, in the middle of the night with a gigantic winch that had a boat attached to it. When people made jokes about catching sea monsters, Kelvin only smiled. No one knew what he knew. How could they?

Kevin Kelvin was fishing for teeny-tiny bits of electricity flowing up his Wire. The Wire traveled under the ocean for miles, all the way to a little building on the shore, not far from the lighthouse. He twiddled dials, and listened carefully to a nearby speaker connected to the Wire, and made notes. If his ideas were right, any moment now he should hear a signal from his assistant on the other end. It would sound like—

BEEP.

His skin tingled with excitement, but he didn't dare make a sound.

BLOOP. BEEP.

Kelvin quickly disconnected some wires and connected some other ones. He flicked a switch on and off.

FLIP. FLOP. FLIP.

The Wire answered back.

BLOOP.

The Wire worked! Just as Kelvin thought: he could send messages using electricity, even under miles of seawater. If the *Jargonaut* laid down a Wire all the way between two islands, that would form the first link in Kelvin's very own Network. A Network that could send messages all the time, even on a terrible night like this. A Network that, someday, could even have *multiple Wires.*

Those fools up there in their ivory towers, flashing their little lights, will never know what hit them!

The Field Guide to Userland

You might have wondered whether this or that part of the story is real. Can you really make a Fair Coin out of an Unfair Coin? Can you really use ants to find shorter paths? Yes, you can do both—and a lot more besides. In this guide, you'll find out how some of the places, people, and things Laurie encounters in Userland connect with our own world.

CHAPTER 0: MOSTLY LOST

Jargon   In the real world, jargon doesn't look like a mouse-dog, or even a dog-mouse; it looks just like an ordinary word! Computer scientists (and really, all scientists) love inventing new words. We call these specialized words *jargon* or *argot*. Jargon can be good, because it saves time when you're discussing things with your colleagues. It can also be bad, because it excludes nonexperts from the conversation.

When you're just starting out with programming, all the jargon, argot, and weird new words can be intimidating, but don't let that stop you from learning. Jargon can be silly, or powerful, or dangerous, depending on how you use it. But no matter what words you use, if you always obfuscate instead of explicate, no one will understand you!

Wandering Salesman   The *Traveling Salesman problem* is a classic computer science question. Given a group of cities, your goal is to find the shortest *Hamiltonian path*, a route that lets you visit each city only once. If you have a large number of cities, it would take a very long time to calculate that path, even for a computer. So the Wandering Salesman might be on the road for quite a while!

Instead of calculating the exact answer, the salesman looks for a path through all the towns that's *close enough* to being the shortest. A very interesting aspect of the Traveling Salesman problem is that humans are pretty good at solving small examples by hand. There is much discussion about what algorithm people use in their heads while solving it. See also *Hugh Rustic* (Chapter 8; page 170).

The Upper and Lower Bounds   In Userland, the Upper Bounds are a mountain range, as tall as anything can be. The Lower Bounds are valleys as low and deep as anything can be. Nothing can be higher and nothing can be lower than these two bounds.

In the real world, finding an upper and lower limit on a problem can simplify things a lot. Say you have to guess a person's age. It's unlikely that anyone is over 150 years old, and no one can be younger than 0 years old. So, 150 is the *upper limit* and 0 is the *lower limit*. You can narrow down the bounds even more with simple questions. Is the person still in school? If so, then he is probably younger than 30. Can the person drive a car? If so, then he is probably older than 15.

Mile Zero You sometimes see signs that mark a point on a highway, like "Mile 14." Now, if there is a Mile 14, then there must be a Mile 13, and a Mile 12, and so on. Everything has to start somewhere, and Zero is where it starts. Possibly the most famous Mile Zero is in Key West, Florida. It's at the beginning of US Route 1, which goes all the way to Canada. If you look carefully and are very lucky, you might find a Mile Zero near where you live.

CHAPTER 1: A HIDDEN ALLY

Xor When you say "A or B," you mean that you want one of those two things, or maybe both! If you say "A xor B," then you mean you want *one and only one* of those two things, not both. That's why Xor keeps turning rainbow colors: Xor and the thing he's currently resting on can't be blue at the same time. If he's sitting on a blue sign, then he must turn any color that *isn't* blue! Not a great form of camouflage, is it?

Steganosaurus *Steganography* is the art of hiding information inside other information, and it's used in both the digital and the physical world. For example, you might hide a secret message by writing it with invisible ink on a piece of paper. With a computer program, you could even hide words inside sounds and pictures. A Steganosaurus is, therefore, a dinosaur that can hide itself anywhere.

CHAPTER 2: SENSE AND SENSIBLENESS

Composing Eponymous Bach is a composer, but she works with ideas instead of music. *Composing* is the act of combining small ideas into bigger ones to solve a problem in steps. Almost every idea is composed of smaller ideas. For example, multiplying whole numbers isn't anything special. You can think of it as adding a number to itself and repeating:

2 × 3 = 6
2 + 2 + 2 = 6 (Add up three twos.)

See also *Decomposing* (Chapter 17; page 178) and *Relating* (Chapter 17; page 179). Composing, decomposing, and relating are problem-solving methods that lie at the root of all math, logic, and computer science.

Bach's First Law of Eponymy   Don't let any new idea escape without putting a name on it. A name is like a handle that makes the idea easier to use.

Bach's Second Law of Eponymy   It's better to put a name on Ideas than on Things, because Ideas last longer.

Bach's Third Law of Eponymy
As an idea becomes more useful and famous, its name becomes shorter and lowercase. This law eventually affected Eponymous's friend, Andy Ampère, and his discovery about electricity.

Ampère   André-Marie Ampère discovered that when electricity flows through parallel wires, the wires will either attract or repel each other, causing the wires to bend. By measuring how much they bend, you can measure how much electricity is flowing. Ampère used this idea to lay the foundation for nearly everything we know about electricity, and we measure electrical current in *amperes* (or *amps*) in his honor. (See *Bach's Third Law of Eponymy* for Eponymous's theory on why we don't call the unit an *Ampère* nearly as often.)

Sense vs. Sensibleness Programmers and mathematicians sometimes use a pair of ideas, called the *solution space* and the *problem space*, to describe finding an answer to a problem.

Say you need to move a heavy box so you can unpack it; anything related to moving the box is in your problem space. Try to imagine every single thing you could possibly do to try to move that box. You could walk forward, walk backward, stick out your tongue, sing a song, write an equation, use a lever, call for help, look for a forklift, or do literally anything else you can think of. Write down as many of these possibilities as you can fit on a piece of paper.

Out of that huge space of possibilities, imagine only the ones that have a good chance of moving the box. Circle those with a red pen. The circled ones are in the solution space. They *make sense* because they would accomplish your goal, and the rest don't make sense. Now, look again at all of the circled possibilities and think about which one is best (fastest, cheapest, easiest, most reliable, and so on). Underline that one in green. That's the most *sensible* answer out of all the ones that make sense.

The point of this exercise is to avoid a very human, very common error: we tend to grasp at the first solution we think of and forget to consider other possibilities. This is what Eponymous means when she tells Laurie that the Wandering Salesman's solution isn't sensible. See also *Hugh Rustic* (Chapter 8; page 170) and *Five Whys* (Chapter 14; page 175).

CHAPTER 3: ROUNDING ERROR

Round Robin Algorithm The Robins aren't really evil—they're just hungry. They cooperate in everything they do, taking turns and making sure the work is balanced among them. Sharing work is a great way to get things done faster, and computers can share work, too!

You can find the Round Robin method almost anywhere. Imagine a bus route that takes an hour to complete. If you put two buses on that route, a bus will arrive at each stop every 30 minutes. With three buses, you'd see a bus every 20 minutes, and four means you'd see one every 15 minutes. With five buses, you'd see one every 12 minutes, and so on. Just divide 60 (the number of minutes in an hour) by the number of buses to see how often a bus should come.

But you have to be careful to make sure the buses arrive at each stop at evenly spaced times. Five buses reaching one stop all at once wouldn't be balanced. Also, if one bus breaks down and gets delayed, this could cause all the other buses to back up!

CHAPTER 4: WHAT THE TORTOISE SAID TO LAURIE

Recursion *Recursion* is a way to repeat the same process over and over until you find the answer you're looking for. When you use recursion, you run though the process, and if the answer is the one you want, you stop. If it's not, you take the answer you found, plug it into the same process, and run it again.

Let's look at an example of recursion in action right here in Userland. Recall from Chapter 10 that Jane Hecate has a single, gigantic book of names. The name *Lauren* starts with *L*, so Jane should find it in the *L* section of her book, but that could take a while with so many pages. If Jane wants a faster way to look for *Lauren*, she can divide the book into two equal halves and see if *L* is in the first half or the second half.

First half: {A, B, C, D, E, F, G, H, I, J, K, L, M}
Second half: {N, O, P, Q, R, S, T, U, V, W, X, Y, Z}

Since *L* is in the first half, Jane can then divide the first half of the book in half, giving her two quarters of the book to search.

First quarter: {A, B, C, D, E, F, G}
Second quarter: {H, I, J, K, L, M}

Lauren should be in the second quarter, so Jane can divide that quarter in half, giving her two eighths of the alphabet:

First eighth: {H, I, J}
Second eighth: {K, L, M}

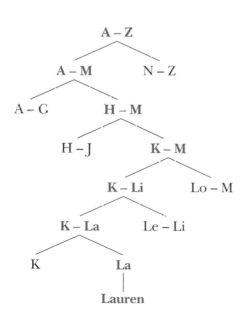

Jane can continue dividing the letter groups containing *L* in half until eventually she ends up with just the *L* section. (How many more times would Jane have to divide a set of letters in half to find *L*?) This way of searching for a particular piece of information is called a *binary search*.

See also *The Garden of Forking Paths* (Chapter 19; page 181) and *Chasing Your Tail* (page 162).

Achilles and the Tortoise   These two characters were used by a philosopher named Zeno of Elea almost 2,500 years ago to talk about infinity. From Aristotle to Lewis Carroll to Marvin Minsky to Douglas Hofstadter, mathematics is full of stories about their adventures. It's Tortoises all the way down.

Chasing Your Tail   Chasing your own tail is not always a waste of time! In computer science, there's a type of recursion that sounds a bit like running around in circles, and it's quite useful. In *tail recursion*, you perform a process, then perform the process again on the result, and repeat until you reach the final answer. For example, Jane Hecate's binary search for the *L* section of her book might look something like this:

- Check the section of the book of names we have right now.
- Do we only have the *L* section?
- If so, then we're done!
- If not, then divide the book in half.
- Look at the half of the list containing the *L* section, and repeat.

See also *Recursion* (page 160).

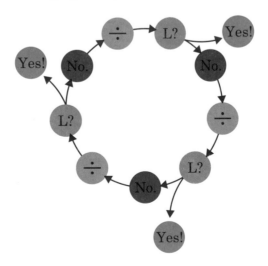

Infinity   When people say there's an *infinite* amount of something, they mean there's no limit to how much of that thing exists. When Tortoise demonstrates how an infinite string can be less than two inches long, he shows that you can split that string into an infinite number of smaller pieces.

Infinity is *big*, bigger than you can imagine. But you can hold infinity in your mind simply by saying a few words. There are infinite odd numbers: 1, 3, 5, 7, and so on, up to forever. There are infinite even numbers, too: 0, 2, 4, 6, 8, and so on. No matter how hard you look, you will never find an odd number in the list of even numbers or an even number among the odd ones. That means there are at least two kinds of infinity: the even numbers and the odd numbers.

There are also *infinite kinds of infinity*. Think about all the numbers divisible by 3 and all the numbers *not* divisible by 3 (or 4, or 5). Now imagine all the numbers that no one else has thought of before. That's another kind of infinity!

Infinite Regress   If you think about how you think, you might then start thinking about how you think about how you think, and then about how you think about how you think about how you think, and so on. This is a form of argument called *infinite regress*, and it can have no end. The first time you fall into this mental trap, it can be confusing or even scary. The trick is not to take it too seriously.

If you think this sounds related to recursion, you're correct! It would be quite troubling to get stuck in a recursive process forever. In real computers, infinite recursion never actually happens because no computer can hold an infinite amount of information. When the computer runs out of room while working on something recursive, you never know what might happen. Laurie and Xor experienced this firsthand at Recursion Junction. See also *Chasing Your Tail* (page 162).

CHAPTER 5: WELCOME TO SYMBOL

Semantic Turnstile ⊨ is a logical symbol that points the way to a truth. It's kind of like the equal sign (=), except that it shows how *ideas* are related instead of numbers. If all the ideas to the left of the semantic turnstile are true, then the idea on the right is also true.

Say you have two ideas: (A) "You have the password" and (B) "You may enter." You can compose these ideas together to make a *rule*:

(A → B)   "IF you have the password, THEN you may enter."

That is the rule that Ponens explained to Laurie at the gates of Symbol. (Placing two ideas on either side of that little arrow is another way to say, "IF A is true, THEN B is true.")

But how do you know the rule is true? Maybe that's not how you enter Symbol. So you have to show that both the rule (A → B), and the first idea, A, are true. In this case, we need to be sure that both the rule ("IF you have the password, THEN you may enter") and the idea ("You have the password") are true before we let anyone through the gate.

That's what the semantic turnstile is for. We put the rule and the first idea on the left of the turnstile, and put the second idea (B, which is "You may enter" in this case) on the right:

$$(A \rightarrow B), (A) \vDash (B)$$

This means "IF our rule is true and IF you actually have the password, THEN you may enter."

Here's the weirder part: you might have noticed that the turnstile looks a lot like an IF...THEN. IF everything to the left is true, THEN the idea on the right is true. So how do we know this rule as a whole is true? Do we need a turnstile for the turnstile?

$$(A \rightarrow B), (A) \vDash (B) \vDash (C)$$

. . . and then a turnstile for that one, and for the next one?

$$(A \rightarrow B), (A) \vDash (B) \vDash (C) \vDash (D) \vDash (E) \vDash (F) \vDash (G) \ldots$$

In theory, you have to pass an infinite number of turnstiles before you know anything is true! It's a wonder we are able to put our shoes on in the morning! So how do we know that anything is true? How do you know your milk will come out of the carton at breakfast tomorrow, or that your classroom won't be on the roof when you get to school?

In practice, we simply trust that the rules we live by are true, since we've seen them work in the past. However, it can be fun and useful to poke into the rules, as Laurie did. Even if they turn out to make sense, you learn a lot about how they work. Poking at rules is a big part of what science is all about! See *Infinite Regress* (Chapter 4; page 163) and *It's Only Logical* (page 167).

Ponens   His full name is Modus Ponendo Ponens, and he represents a type of logical argument. This type of argument can come to a *logical* conclusion, but that conclusion might not always be *true*. For example, here's how Ponens decided that the gate to Symbol is secure:

- If only people with passwords can enter, then our door is secure.
- Only people with passwords have entered.
- Therefore, our door is secure.

This conclusion may seem logical, but it's not necessarily true. Logic is only as good as the assumptions it depends on. Someone, like Laurie, can *say* she is Eponymous Bach without *actually* being Eponymous Bach, and as long as she has the right password, she can waltz right into Symbol. In that case, all of the logic in the world won't make that gate secure! See also *Tollens* (next) and *Semantic Turnstile* (page 164).

Tollens   His full name is Modus Tollendo Tollens, and, like Ponens, he represents a type of logical argument. In fact, Tollens works a lot like Ponens, but backward. For example, here's how Tollens might decide that his door is secure:

- If our door was insecure, then people without passwords would enter.
- No one without a password has entered.
- Therefore, our door is secure.

This is how Tollens would decide Steganosauruses don't exist:

- If Steganosauruses existed, you would see them.
- You have never seen a Steganosaurus.
- Therefore, they do not exist.

Like Ponens, Modus Tollendo Tollens is perfectly valid logic, but it's only as good as the assumptions it's based on. Just because you don't have proof that something is true, that doesn't mean it's automatically false, and just because you've never seen a Steganosaurus, that doesn't mean they don't exist. Maybe they live on an island you've never been to, or maybe they are so good at hiding that no one can see them. See *It's Only Logical* (next).

It's Only Logical   Even if an idea is logical, it might not be true. It's easy for an idea to be simple, logical, and *false*—if you forget to consider all of the facts. For example, people who go swimming have wet hair when they're finished. If you see someone with wet hair, does that mean she just got out of the pool? No! Perhaps it was raining outside, or maybe she just took a shower.

It's also easy for logic to get stuck in endless loops. See *Ponens* (page 165) and *Infinite Regress* (Chapter 4; page 163).

CHAPTER 6: A TINKER'S TRADE

Algorithm   An *algorithm* is a set of specific steps that you can follow to solve a problem. For example, a recipe for how to make pizza is an algorithm:

1. Spread the dough into a pan.
2. Cover the dough in a layer of pizza sauce.
3. Sprinkle cheese on top of the sauce.
4. Bake the pizza for 20 minutes at 350 degrees Fahrenheit.
5. Take the pizza out of the oven and let it cool.
6. Dig in!

Just like that recipe, Laurie's turtle drawing poems were algorithms. They broke down the process of drawing a circle into small steps, and the turtle followed those instructions to create circles of any size. If you really want to, you can even think up algorithms for algorithms, which is to say, how to figure out how to figure out how to do something. See *Infinite Regress* (Chapter 4; page 163).

How would you tell Tinker's turtle to draw a triangle of any size, where all three angles have the same number of degrees? (Hint: Those three angles should add up to 180 degrees.)

Hamiltonian Cycle   It's quite fitting that Laurie comes from Hamilton, as her "path back to Hamilton" will be a *Hamiltonian path*. This type of path, named for mathematician William Hamilton, is a route by which a traveler visits every town on a map exactly once. In this book, I use the word *path*, but there is actually a slight difference between a Hamiltonian *path* and a Hamiltonian *cycle*, which is a path that returns to where it started.

On a map with N towns, there are $(N - 1)! \div 2$ cycles. As Tinker said, $x!$ is shorthand for $(x \times (x - 1) \times \ldots \times 2 \times 1)$, so for a map with six towns, you'd have

$$(6 - 1)! \div 2 = 5! \div 2 = (5 \times 4 \times 3 \times 2 \times 1) \div 2 = 60 \text{ cycles!}$$

Finding a cycle is fairly easy because there are so many possibilities; finding a *short* one is the hard part! See also *Wandering Salesman* (Chapter 0; page 156).

Fair Coin   A *Fair Coin* is a coin that has an equal chance of landing with heads or tails facing up when you flip it. Real coins (like Laurie's quarters), however, aren't always perfectly balanced in weight, so in our world, there is no such thing as a perfectly fair coin. But for most coins, the odds of landing with either side up are close

enough to fifty-fifty that we have no problem using a coin flip to choose between two options.

Even so, for important things like physics simulations, or choosing who gets to ride in the front seat, flip twice to guarantee absolute fairness. See also *A Fair Flip* (Chapter 11; page 173).

Circle   When Laurie used the turtle robot to make a circle, she discovered that filling in one for how-big? made a much bigger circle than she expected. What number should you plug into MOTH-CIRCLE in order to draw a circle two inches in diameter?

```
MOTH-CIRCLE (how-big?):
Go forward how-big? inches,
make a mark,
turn right one degree,
repeat three hundred sixty times.

make a MOTH-CIRCLE (how-big?).
```

Improbable vs. Impossible   No matter which subject you study, there will always be problems that just don't have a solution. We say that those problems are *impossible* to solve. Some problems, on the other hand, can be solved, but only under highly unlikely conditions. Those are *improbable*.

CHAPTER 7: READ ME

Cryptography   Thank goodness Xor was able to decode Colonel Trapp's secret message! People have been encoding information into *ciphers* for others to decode since ancient times, and today, that science is called *cryptography*. Computers are great at creating and cracking secret codes, but you can do it, too!

One quick way to encode a message is by using a *substitution cipher*, which is when you replace each letter in your message with something else. For example, you could map each letter to a number:

A	B	C	D	E	F	G	H	I	J	K	L	M	N	O	P	Q	R	S	T	U	V	W	X	Y	Z
0	1	2	3	4	5	6	7	8	9	10	11	12	13	14	15	16	17	18	19	20	21	22	23	24	25

Following these rules, "Hello!" would become "7 4 11 11 14!" But you can replace those letters with anything you want: different numbers, other letters, or even symbols you create yourself. Make your own secret message and see if your friends can crack it. Or, share your cipher with your friends so you can send each other secret messages that no one else can read!

CHAPTER 8: MORE THAN ONE WAY TO DO IT

Hugh Rustic   If there are millions of possible ways to solve a difficult problem, searching for the best solution just isn't practical. When that happens, scientists use *heuristics* to find an answer that is, as Hugh Rustic might say, "good enough."

Heuristic algorithms are based on experience—on things that we know will work—but they aren't guaranteed to be the best possible solutions. For example, Hugh Rustic's ants find many different paths on the map at random, and by following the scent trails of other ants. Scent trails eventually dry up if no new ants follow them. The shorter a path is, the more ants follow it, which makes the scent stronger. Over time, shorter paths become more popular and longer ones fade away. Based on what Laurie saw the ants do, she knows the path is short, even if it may not be the shortest, so she can use that as a heuristic to get home more quickly.

Something to think about: Is Hugh Rustic's ant map through Userland the shortest possible path, or is it only a short-enough path? Can you do better? Try it!

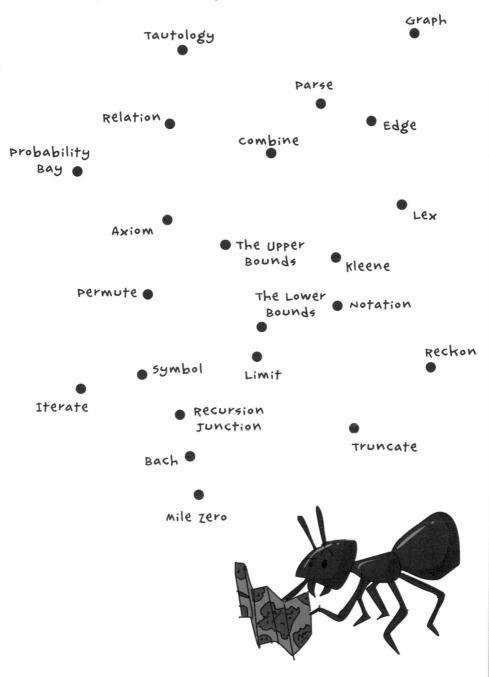

CHAPTER 9: DON'T REPEAT YOURSELF

Axiom Much as Xor said, an *axiom* is a rule or principle that you can't prove, but that everyone accepts as true because it just makes sense. Mathematicians, scientists, and anyone who wants to prove anything might start their argument with an axiom.

For example, the idea that *part* of a thing is always smaller than the *entire* thing is an axiom. If you cut a slice out of a pie, there's no way that slice can be bigger than the whole pie. The same rule applies to numbers: if you take 2 away from 5, you're left holding a 2 and a 3, and neither is more than 5.

CHAPTER 10: A WELL-TIMED ENTRANCE

Timing Attack Jane Hecate checks each letter of Laurie's password guesses one by one until there is a mismatch with the correct password. The more letters Laurie gets correct in a row, the longer it takes for Jane to find a mismatch, which tells Laurie how close her guess is to being right.

Computer scientists call this a *timing attack* because the guesser watches the amount of time it takes to check each incorrect try and makes new guesses based on that. Many people who should know better make Jane's mistake and leak information about the secret they are keeping.

CHAPTER 11: A FAIR EXCHANGE

A Fair Flip   As Trent Escrow explains to Laurie, you can guarantee a fifty-fifty chance of flipping heads or tails on an unbalanced coin—if you flip it twice. If you get Heads-Tails, then Heads is your answer. If you get Tails-Heads, then Tails is your answer. At least half of the time, you'll probably flip Heads-Heads or Tails-Tails; in those cases, just start over. On average, you'll need at least three coin flips to get a Fair flip. Try it! See also *Fair Coin* (Chapter 6; page 168).

CHAPTER 12: AN IMPROBABLE TWIST

Attempted Mythology . . . is not actually a crime in any jurisdiction, and that's a good thing! Otherwise, no one would be allowed to write any stories, and *myths* are just stories that have been passed down to us through many generations. Some myths try to explain how the world works, and some are just for fun. Use your imagination, and maybe someday, you'll write a story that becomes part of a future mythology.

The *Doppelganger*   The *Doppelganger*'s tale is based on a classic question in philosophy: If you replace all of the parts of a boat, do you still have the same boat? Winsome doesn't think so. She claims she stole the *Doppelganger* from its owner piece by piece and left him with a copy! But what do you think? If you reassemble the old parts, which boat is the original? What if you replaced only half of the parts?

Gliders *Conway's Game of Life* is a simulation of how a population of creatures might change over time. Computer scientists (and plenty of other scientists) use the Game of Life to study patterns based on simple rules. You can try it out yourself with a pencil and paper! First, grab some graph paper or draw a grid like this:

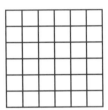

Now fill in some squares in the grid. Here's one example:

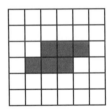

After you've filled in some squares, you just have to follow a few simple rules to play the game and change your pattern:

1. If a filled-in square has more than three filled-in neighbors, then it dies. Make it blank.
2. If a filled-in square has only one or zero filled-in neighbors, it dies. Make it blank.
3. If a filled-in square has two or three filled-in neighbors, it survives! Leave it colored in.
4. If a blank square has three filled-in neighbors, it comes to life! Color it in.

Follow these rules to color in a new grid. Our sample grid would turn out like this after one round:

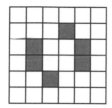

These patterns come in many types. *Gliders* move around. *Blinkers* turn on and off, like traffic lights. Some patterns even create other patterns as they go. This particular grid pattern repeats:

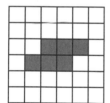 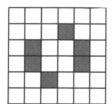 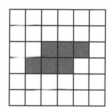

CHAPTER 14: IN THE ABSTRACT

Five Whys When scientists want to get to the root cause of a confusing problem, they'll ask Why questions until they find out exactly Where their experiment went Wrong. But you don't have to leave that kind of thinking to the scientists.

Play Five Whys the next time you need to figure out the solution to a problem of your own. There are a lot of mental games you can try to help you avoid or learn from mistakes. Another good rule is "Never worry alone." Grab a friend if you're puzzled—when you work together, you can solve any problem!

Following the Byzantine Process The word *Byzantine* can describe any extremely long and complicated process. Fortunately, Laurie was able to get all of the signatures she needed by helping the three generals, and she actually solved each of their very different problems similarly.

Laurie's algorithm for moving the wolf, the goat, and the mandelbroccoli uses a *counting argument*. The idea behind a counting argument is that you can solve some problems by ignoring unimportant differences between things and counting only how many there are. For example:

- Everyone wants to use General Euripides's books all at once. But reader or writer, only *one* person can use any given book at a time.
- General Darius was so concerned with getting the mandelbroccoli, the wolf, and the goat across the stream that he didn't think of counting backward—of bringing the goat across *multiple times*. But mandelbroccoli or wolf, as long as you don't leave the goat alone with it, everything works out.

Sometimes it's the opposite: you have to count the same thing different ways to see if they add up. General Case stopped counting posts after he hit 100 feet of fence; he wasn't thinking about holding up the last length! Count the gaps *between* the posts and you get 10. Count the *posts*, and you get 11.

When Tinker tells Laurie to count paths that are mirror images of other paths (like BCD and DCB) as one, he is also using a counting argument. This rule cuts the number of paths through Userland in half. But even cutting the number in half doesn't help much with the Traveling Salesman problem: a Very Big Number divided by a small number is still a Very Big Number!

Mandelbroccoli Mandelbroccoli does exist in our world, and it's the weirdest-looking vegetable I know. At the market, it's called *Romanesco*, and it looks a lot like a fractal. *Fractals* are patterns that start with one shape and repeat it infinitely, smaller and smaller, according to a set of rules.

For example, draw an equilateral triangle (a triangle with three sides that are all the same length) inside another equilateral triangle. Make sure each point from the second triangle touches the middle of a side from the first! This should create four smaller, but identical, triangles inside the original.

Now, draw an equilateral triangle inside each of those, following the same rules, and repeat until you can't fit any more triangles. You should have something like the fractal pattern shown here. See also *Infinity* (Chapter 4; page 163).

"Sierpinski triangle evolution." Licensed under public domain via Wikimedia Commons.

CHAPTER 16: A CHANGE OF PLAN

Bruto Fuerza This lighthouse keeper thinks the answer to every problem is more power and brute force. Even if he builds a lighthouse twice as tall, twice as wide, and twice as thick as the one that failed, the new one will still fall over eventually because he's following the same plan.

Yet in his own way, Bruto is right when he decides to build a pyramid instead. Pyramids are much sturdier, and if you pile on enough bricks, you could eventually make a pyramid tall enough to be a lighthouse. But Bruto's plan has enormous costs: he needs a lot more bricks, a lot more land to build on, and a lot more time to build.

Some programmers approach problems this way, too, but putting all your resources into a brute-force attempt isn't always a sensible answer. When your algorithm collapses, don't just pile on more bricks! Change your point of view, as Laurie did with the generals on the Island of Byzantium, and you'll find a more effective solution. See also *Five Whys* (Chapter 14; page 175).

CHAPTER 17: CHASING ELEGANTS

Elegants   They don't really exist, but don't you wish they did?

Fresnel   The Fresnel whom Laurie meets on Elegant Island is named after a real scientist named Augustin-Jean Fresnel, who invented a way of focusing big lighthouse lights with only a little bit of glass. He knew that lenses didn't have to be large and thick to focus a beam of light, so instead of one huge piece of glass, the *Fresnel lens* is an arrangement of small pieces of glass at different angles. Lighthouses still use this type of lens today.

Decomposing   *Decomposing* starts with a big idea and breaks it into smaller, easier-to-understand pieces. When you know how to solve each smaller piece, you can combine those ideas to solve a bigger problem. One good way to take an idea apart is to describe it without using its name, just as Laurie did when she said you could also call a turtle a "Green Round animal with a Shell."

Even simple ideas, like the numbers 3 and 4, can be decomposed into simpler ideas. Start with 0 and then add 1. Then add 1 again, and so on:

$$0 = 0$$
$$1 = 0 + 1$$
$$2 = 0 + 1 + 1$$
$$3 = 0 + 1 + 1 + 1$$

If you really wanted to, you could just use 0 and 1 and ditch all of the other numbers. I don't recommend it—you'll use up a lot of paper!—but it's a perfectly valid way to do math. For example, let's break an addition problem down into nothing but 0s and 1s:

$$2 + 2 = 4$$

would become

$$(0 + 1 + 1) + (0 + 1 + 1) = (0 + 1 + 1 + 1 + 1)$$

Relating When you *relate* two ideas, you put them side by side and compare them, like Fresnel's balloon and a lighthouse. With numbers, you use the less-than sign (<) to show that the number on the left is smaller than the one on the right. You use the equal sign (=) to show that the value on the left is equal to the value on the right.

$$2 < 3$$
$$2 \times 3 = 6$$

You can relate things besides numbers, though that means some relations are less precise. Fresnel's balloon isn't *exactly* a lighthouse, but it's *like* a lighthouse. We expect a lighthouse to have a way for people to climb up high, somewhere to stand when they get there, and a big light that faraway ships can see. Fresnel's balloon technically has all of those things:

- Fresnel's balloon *is-like-a* lighthouse.
- (elevator, balloon, light) *is-like-a* (staircase, tower, light).

CHAPTER 18: MANY HANDS MAKE LIGHT WORK

Network   Winsome created the Lighthouse Network to let people in Userland send messages faster. In computer science, a *network* is a group of computers that are connected to one another so that they can share information. Those computers could be connected through wires or even the air!

Baudot   In 1870, Émile Baudot invented a code that represented letters with different groups of 1s and 0s. This code was meant to let people share messages using electricity: if you have a switch, the power can either be on (1) or off (0). Naturally, Baudot named this code after himself. See *Bach's Laws of Eponymy* (Chapter 2; page 158).

We don't use the Baudot code very often in the real world, but Ping, Fresnel, and the other members of Winsome's Lighthouse Network use it to send messages with their lights, which can also be on (FLASH) or off (FLOOSH).

Here's the Baudot code and the letter each number stands for, so you can make your own Lighthouse Network. Grab some friends and some flashlights, and send each other messages!

Letter	Baudot code	Letter	Baudot code
A	11000	N	00110
B	10011	O	00011
C	01110	P	01101
D	10010	Q	11101
E	10000	R	01010
F	10110	S	10100
G	01011	T	00001
H	00101	U	11100
I	01100	V	01111
J	11010	W	11001
K	11110	X	10111
L	01001	Y	10101
M	00111	Z	10001

CHAPTER 19: BRANCHING OUT

The Garden of Forking Paths   The Garden has 16,777,216 paths, but in the end, Laurie and Xor each found exactly one path that made sense for them. The number of possible paths became so small so fast because at each fork, Laurie answered an either/or question, and that cut the number of possible paths in half.

Laurie's journey through the Garden of Forking Paths is a lot like what computer scientists call a *binary search*, which programmers use to look for a single piece of information in a huge list quickly. When something is binary, it has only two parts— just like the questions the Garden asked Laurie.

This little chart has four possible outcomes. If you answer the question "A or B?" with A, you cut that number in half, leaving only two possibilities. Then, at A, you have to answer "C or D?" Whichever option you pick, you're cutting the number in half again, to one choice.

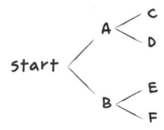

In a binary search, you would ask similar questions about your giant list of information; eventually, you'd cut the possibilities down to just one. Try it the next time you play Twenty Questions! If you choose your questions (or answers) carefully, you can arrive at virtually anything in only 20 or 30 steps. See also *Recursion* (Chapter 4; page 160).

CHAPTER **21**: ONE MORE THING

Telegraph   Captain Kevin Kelvin is laying wire along the ocean to create a *telegraph* network. Telegraph systems let people send messages to one another over long distances without actually sending a physical object. Winsome's Lighthouse Network is also a type of telegraph!

In Kevin's case, letters are represented by collections of sounds, not lights. Different combinations of beeps and bloops represent different letters, and those beeps and bloops are made when Kevin's assistant presses a button attached to the other end of the wire. The telegraph is just one of many systems people have used throughout history to talk to one another.

Kelvin Scale   Lord Kelvin was a real engineer who worked on telegraphs, but he's best known for creating the Kelvin scale to measure temperature. Unlike other temperature scales, the Kelvin scale doesn't use numbers less than zero, so the coldest temperature that anything can be is called *absolute zero*. Water freezes into ice at a whopping 273.16 Kelvin!

MORE SMART BOOKS
FOR CURIOUS KIDS!

no starch press

PYTHON FOR KIDS
A PLAYFUL INTRODUCTION TO PROGRAMMING
by JASON R. BRIGGS
DEC 2012, 344 PP., $34.95
ISBN 978-1-59327-407-8
full color

RUBY WIZARDRY
AN INTRODUCTION TO PROGRAMMING FOR KIDS
by ERIC WEINSTEIN
DEC 2014, 360 PP., $29.95
ISBN 978-1-59327-566-2
two color

JAVASCRIPT FOR KIDS
A PLAYFUL INTRODUCTION TO PROGRAMMING
by NICK MORGAN
DEC 2014, 348 PP., $34.95
ISBN 978-1-59327-408-5
full color

SURVIVE! INSIDE THE HUMAN BODY, VOL. 1
THE DIGESTIVE SYSTEM
by GOMDORI CO. *and* HYUN-DONG HAN
OCT 2013, 184 PP., $17.95
ISBN 978-1-59327-471-9
full color

SUPER SCRATCH PROGRAMMING ADVENTURE!
LEARN TO PROGRAM BY MAKING COOL GAMES
by THE LEAD PROJECT
OCT 2013, 160 PP., $24.95
ISBN 978-1-59327-531-0
full color
(Covers Version 2)

LEARN TO PROGRAM WITH SCRATCH
A VISUAL INTRODUCTION TO PROGRAMMING WITH GAMES, ART, SCIENCE, AND MATH
by MAJED MARJI
FEB 2014, 288 PP., $34.95
ISBN 978-1-59327-543-3
full color